PITTSBURGH–THE PORT TO THE WEST

AN ILLUSTRATED HISTORY
ABOUT
THE PEOPLE AND EVENTS
IN PITTSBURGH, PENNSYLVANIA
DURING ITS FIRST ONE HUNDRED YEARS

• Forks of the Ohio

Written & Illustrated by

Denise L. Fantazier

Layout, Book Design & Edited by

Robert J. Fantazier

First Edition
December, 2010
Pittsburgh, Pennsylvania

Manufactured in the United States of America
ISBN 978-0-9831607-0-0
Library of Congress Control Number: 2010917184
Inquiries should be addressed to:

Denise L. Fantazier
P.O. Box 41056
Pittsburgh, PA 15202

Contents

Main Illustrations

Credits

Use of the following photo images has been granted by Library and Archives Division, Historical Society of Western Pennsylvania, Pittsburgh, Pennsylvania:

Page 24   Map of Ohio River from 1818 edition of *The Navigator* by Zadok Cramer.

Page 26   Front cover of *The Navigator*, 1818 edition by Zadok Cramer.

Page 27   Cramer's *Pittsburgh 1822 Almanack* by Zadok Cramer.

Page 39   Keelboat Bill of Lading.

Use of the following photo images has been granted by the Pittsburgh Photographic Library of Carnegie Library of Pittsburgh, Pittsburgh, Pennsylvania:

Page 42   Map of Depreciation Lands

Page 51   Masthead of *The Mystery* by Martin Delany.

The image of George Washington and Christopher Gist crossing the Allegheny on Page 8 is from an original engraving in the author's collection. It was engraved by D. Kimberly from a painting by D. Huntington.

The Map of the Forks of the Ohio and Journal Page on Page 9 are reproduced from George Washington's Journal—the Report he made to the Governor of Virginia in 1754.

Also, the digital images in this edition were made by the author and her husband.

Acknowledgements

Special thanks to Archaeologist Richard Lang for his expert advice on the physical layout and construction of Fort Pitt. He described, in great detail, what the Fort looked like in 1763. He also identified the possible locations where the women in the bucket brigade painting (Page 20) stood to effectively aim the small "water engine" at the burning roof of the Commandant's house. This fire had been started by flaming arrows coming into the Fort.

Thanks also to Kelly Linn, Curator of the Fort Pitt Block House, for her review of content of this book.

Thanks to Gil Pietrzak at Carnegie Library of Pittsburgh, and to Art Louderback at the Library and Archives Division, Historical Society of Western Pennsylvania located at the Senator John Heinz History Museum, for their assistance in obtaining permission to use various images in this book.

Thanks to Greg Priore, Archivist for Carnegie Library Special Archive Collection, who assisted the research of early volunteer fire companies in Pittsburgh, PA.

Thanks to Chris Gaul for performing a final edit of this book. Thanks also to Karen Gaul, Amy Skelly, Jill Fetzer and Jonathan Fantazier for their suggestions and advice as educators.

Thanks to the many local reenactors who have participated in several recent years of historic events in various locations. Their willingness to model what people looked like a few hundred years ago was a visual inspiration for my paintings.

Thanks also to my family, both living and dead, who also provided reference for the characters in these illustrations.

I was raised in a family who taught by example the importance of giving 100% effort to the work of their hands. The great work ethic that they practiced came from a continuation of pioneer perseverance. Pittsburgh families are known for nuturing dedicated, hard-working people. I'm proud to say that my own children are prime examples of this standard of achievement.

My greatest thanks needs to be to my husband. He has supported, encouraged, enabled, and helped produce this work. His great talents and abilities as a graphic artist and editor have allowed my words and paintings to blossom into this book.

Denise Fantazier

Preface

When my husband and I visited Williamsburg, Virginia, for the first time in 2004, I was astounded by the power that history could give to a location. Besides the handsomely restored architecture, there were dedicated reenactors, who not only dressed the part but were reliving the actual daily lives of earlier residents of that town. The gifted and talented reenactor craftsmen and craftswomen were creating actual objects used by the people of the 1700's, using traditional early processes. There were amazing lectures by knowledgeable spirits of formidable men of the day like "Patrick Henry," followed by unscripted question and answer periods. The original Tavern/ Inns (now Restaurants) that served delicious food with authentic flair reinforced the step back in time. It was the spirit of all of these things together that imbued a startling realization that I wasn't just there in the here and now, but instead simultaneously felt transported in time to that earlier environment.

It was an anachronistic experience.

My immediate reaction was to ask, "Could the people of Pittsburgh do this?" Could we create a living history venue to show the importance of what happened here?

In Pittsburgh, we live on sacred ground. Young George Washington foresaw this as the place for controlling use of the rivers. George recognized the Forks of the Ohio (Pittsburgh), as the command location that could control travel from the east coast to the interior of the American continent.

In trying to establish English control of the Forks, George participated in the beginning and end of what became known as The French and Indian War. The natural resources and pristine beauty of the Ohio Valley were a magnet that drew a multitude of pioneers and the British and French into a fight for the gateway to the rest of the continent. In the 1700's, there were no roads, railroads or other methods of transportation to go from colonial civilization in the east to future cities in the Midwest and western parts of America. The best way to get there was through Pittsburgh and down the Ohio River.

Knowing the history in Pittsburgh, I wanted to illustrate how people lived, and share how important this place was for our country. I hope that adults and children learn why Pittsburgh is a historic destination. Pittsburgh was both the port to the west, and to the rest of America.

Denise Fantazier

This Indenture

Witness that in the Twenty-ninth year of the reign of our Sovereign Lord George, by the Grace of God King of England Scotland Ireland defender of the faith &c. on the twenty-ninth day of July Anno Domine 1755 that Jonathan Stephen a laborer doth voluntarily put himself Servant to Robert Joseph his Executors from this day until the said Jonathan Stephen's arrival in Philadelphia in AMERICA. Wherein at that time, Jonathan Stephen shall truly serve the said Robert Joseph his Executors and assigns in his Plantation in Pennsylvania beyond the Seas, for the space of Four Years. Jonathan Stephen now to be the age of 16 years Single and no Covenant or contracted Servant to any other Person, and he agrees to perform the duties given to him. And the said Robert Joseph doth promise and agree at his own proper costs and charges with what convenient speed may carry and convey over onto said Plantation the said Jonathan Stephen and from henceforth and during the said Voyage and also during the said Term shall and will provide for and allow Jonathan Stephen all necessary meat, drink, washing, lodging fit as servants in such cases are usually provided. and Also at the expiration of the said term Jonathan Stephen will receive one new set of clothing, one set of hand tools and Sixty Pounds Sterling.

In Witness whereof John Albert Master of the Sally Jo and representative of Robert Joseph doth sign his hand and witness this above written agreement as also signed by Jonathan Stephen below.

John Albert   *Jonathan Stephen*

Pittsburgh–
The Port to the West

Along the the Atlantic coast of North America, the areas known as the 13 English Colonies were inhabited by many immigrants who came from Europe to live. England gave pieces of land to be colonized as frontier property. People were allowed to settle there, but the Colonies still belonged to the parent state of England.

Native American people had been on the continent since time immemorial.

Vocabulary Words

immigrant
colony
immemorial
ancestors
port

With the arrival of Europeans, the native people suffered a wave of illness from diseases that they'd never experienced before. Many native people died of European diseases without ever having met or seen a European. The Native Americans who survived lived in a very different land than their ancestors, with Europeans and Africans coming to the American Colonies throughout the next two centuries.

The New England colonies included New Hampshire, Massachusetts, Rhode Island, and Connecticut. The Middle colonies included New York, New Jersey, Pennsylvania, and Delaware. The Southern colonies were Maryland, Virginia, North Carolina, South Carolina, and Georgia.[1] It's hard to imagine how difficult it was for those people to come and live in early America. To begin with they had to cross the Atlantic Ocean, a trip that took from six to eight weeks in small wooden sailing ships.

The land in the middle and southern Colonies was excellent for farming. As more and more settlers arrived, the nearest land was taken, and people began to look for their own piece of farmland further west.[2] Going west to settle was hard. The few roads to travel on were in very poor condition. Mountains had to be climbed over. Once across the mountains, the best way to travel further west was to use the rivers. Although most people living in this area today do not see Pittsburgh as a port – not located on an ocean – Pittsburgh, Pennsylvania became the largest inland port in the United States. Here, two rivers came together and were called the "Forks of the Ohio." The Ohio River, which begins in Pittsburgh, allowed people to move to the west by boats. From Pittsburgh, you could travel to the Mississippi River and then all the way to New Orleans. Immigrants and pioneers came here to prepare for their journeys to the open lands in Ohio, Kentucky, Indiana, and further west.

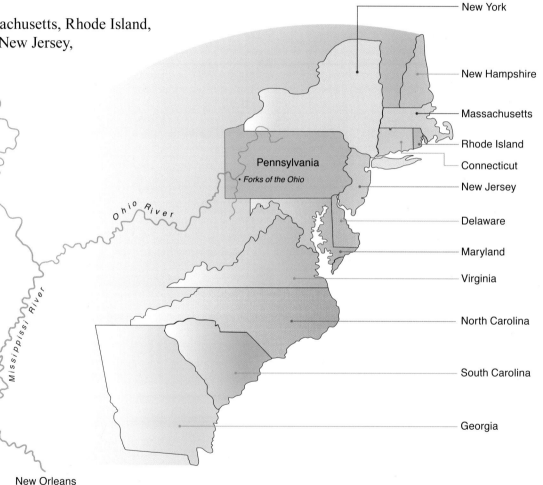

The 13 Original English Colonies in North America

Indentured Servants

Joseph, hat in hand, stood in front of his older brother Robert, waiting their turn to sign the indenture papers. They had no trouble finding a ship in the harbor to sign onto. There were many ships waiting for a full load of passengers before sailing west to America. The ship's Captain sat co-signing the indentures, or contracts. He had made the voyage across the Atlantic many times and knew that he would find a ready market in America for the group in front of him.[3] The cities and plantations in America were waiting for as many workers as would come. By paying the cost of travel for an indentured servant's trip, an owner had free labor from that servant for at least four to six years. The rich farmland in the middle Colonies (New York, New Jersey, Pennsylvania and Delaware) and southern Colonies (Maryland, Virginia, North Carolina, South Carolina and Georgia) produced cash crops that could be sold both in America and back in Europe.

Vocabulary Words

indenture

pioneer

More than half, almost two thirds of immigrants coming to Colonial America, came as indentured servants.[4] During the 1600 and 1700s many poor people in Europe couldn't find work. They heard of jobs in America but couldn't afford the trip to come here. The cost of travel by boat (the only available way to go) was equal to more than half, almost a whole year's worth of their wages (if they had been working). So, instead of paying for their trip in money, they made the journey to America by signing themselves into contracts, or "indentures." The word "indenture" was used to describe the "indented" appearance of the torn, jagged edge contract paper that was signed by both the indentured servant and his/her owner. Each kept their half of the contract to show what had been agreed upon.[5] Most of them came from England, Ireland, Scotland, France, and Germany. By signing indentures, they promised to work for a fixed number of years (usually 4 to 6 years). In return, they were promised a "freedom wage" at the end of their indenture, which included a small amount of money, some clothes (including one new set), and some tools. Most were young (12 to 25 years old) and unmarried. Sometimes entire families, including children, became indentured. Sometimes people became indentured servants unwillingly. They were sold into indentures to repay debts. Orphan children were at times signed into indentures by their villages to reduce the cost of their care. Often prisoners were signed into indentures to get rid of them. People who had committed crimes were put into prisons.[6] However many people were also imprisoned because they could not pay their debts.[7]

The voyage to America for these indentured servants was very difficult. They were given small amounts of food and water that had to last for days, during the six to eight weeks it took to cross the ocean. Most of the time, they weren't allowed freedom to come up on deck. Many became motion sick from the ocean's continual waves; others developed contagious diseases from being locked up in cramped, dirty rooms below deck. Some of them died during the trip. For those that did arrive, they usually had no choice in where they worked. Most indentured servants went to work on large farms called plantations located in the middle and southern Colonies in America. Farming that rich soil, with a long growing season, required many more laborers for a plantation to be successful.[8]

The contract for these servants could be sold or traded from one owner to another.

How much control should property owners have over the lives of indentured servants during their contract?

As indentured servants, these people were owned and had no personal rights. They could not marry. Sometimes they were treated kindly, but too often they were not. When they finally earned their freedom, they traveled west to find their own land. The earliest indenture contracts had included a promise of some land be given to the indentured servant at the end of their service time, but this practice soon ended. Land in the east was too scarce and expensive for the freed servant to buy. Land ownership was very important to them. In Europe there was no chance of improving their wealth or status without owning land and property. Even if you were skilled enough to earn some money, you could never be considered important unless you were born into wealth. After completing their years of indentured work, the pioneers who traveled west usually came on foot, carrying their few belongings. In the American West they finally had the freedom and opportunity to work for a better life.[9]

What would you want to do when your indentured years were finished?

People living in the Southern Colonies soon developed large farms called plantations where their crops needed many laborers for growing, harvesting, and shipping. The Dutch brought the first African people into Jamestown, Virginia in 1619 as indentured servants. Like the European people, who were brought in as field hands, the Africans worked without pay until their indenture time was over. Then they became free landowners. It wasn't until 1662 that this changed. Then more and more African people were brought by force as slaves, instead of as enlisted indentured servants. Many of them and their children became slaves for life.[10]

What do you think changed between 1619 and 1662? Why was the unfair treatment of Africans as slaves allowed to replace their indenture service?

There was another type of indenture in the American colonies. An apprentice signed an indenture contract binding him or her for a length of time to a master craftsman in exchange for being taught a trade. Benjamin Franklin, who became a famous American Patriot during the Revolutionary War, became an indentured apprentice. He was very bright and did well in school, but when he was 10 years old his father could no longer afford to pay for his schooling. Benjamin worked with his father making soap and candles, but he was very bored. Benjamin's father convinced him to indenture himself as an apprentice to his brother James who was a printer. Benjamin worked hard and soon became a very good printer. Benjamin said,

"I signed the indentures when I was yet but twelve years old. I was to serve as an apprentice till I was yet twenty-one years years of age … I now had access to better books." [11]

Benjamin became well educated and eventually was a well-known scientist, writer, and leader of what was to become the United States of America.

Indian Traders

Smiling Star stood close to her mother as they looked around George Croghan's Trading Store. The one room log cabin store was full from top to bottom of wondrous sights. From half of the ceiling rafters on one side of the store hung fur pelts like the ones that Smiling Star's Father and Mother had just carried into the store. Native Americans could trade animal skins for English made goods. Smiling Star had helped her mother scrape fur off of the deer buck skins that would be sent to England and made into leather belts, breeches, purses, and wallets. Indian Fur Traders, like Mr. Croghan, fixed their prices based on a single deer buck skin.[12] In 1761, you could trade four buck skins for a wool blanket. A match coat would trade for three buck skins and a ruffled shirt for four buck skins.[13] This is the origin of our use of the word "buck" to mean a single dollar bill today. The beaver fur was barbed and could be made into felt hats that were water-proof. Smiling Star and her mother were both delighted in looking at reflections of themselves in a small hand mirror in the store. Smiling Star's father carefully inspected a rifle that would make his hunting for pelts easier. The pelts of mink, fox, muskrat, and raccoon were silky and warm. The otter fur was dark and sparkling, soft and shiny.[14]

If you never saw a mirror before, would you trade it for an animal skin that you had spent days in cleaning?

A tree bark wigwam

Vocabulary Words

wigwam

lacrosse

settlers

fur trader

fur pelt

buckskin

Revolutionary War

colonial governor

Once European people started to move into the east coast of North America, the Native Americans were forced to move further west. During the 1700s, the Shawnee, Delaware, and Mingo tribes lived near Pittsburgh. They lived in wigwams made of tree bark that were easy to take down or put up as they moved from one camping area to another. The Seneca and Erie Indians lived further north, closer to Lake Erie. Native American Indians didn't want the Europeans to come further west. Many of them had moved west to allow the Europeans to settle in the colonies along the Atlantic Ocean. Some American Indians had been paid for their land, but most of it had just been taken from them.

On the east bank of the Ohio River, about 18 miles below the Forks of the Ohio near today's Ambridge, was Logstown, the most important Indian village at that time. Here lived Shawnee, Delaware, and Mingo Tribes. Early in the 1700s, French explorers, coming down from Canada, had setup Indian Trading Posts and built Forts in Pennsylvania, Ohio, and Indiana, claiming the land for the French King. By the 1730s, English traders came west from colonial towns along the Atlantic Ocean, believing that this same land should belong to the English King.

These French and English Indian traders came to the Ohio valley in the 1700s to buy fur pelts from the Indians. They were also called "fur traders" because they traded things that the Indians wanted for fur pelts. They lived like the Indians, hunting and trapping and organizing Indian trading. They often married Indian wives. The French and English saw the Indians playing with a ball and webbed sticks. The French Jesuit Priests thought that the webbed sticks to throw and carry the ball looked like a crook used in their church by Catholic bishops. They called the game "le jeu da crosse." Today it is known as lacrosse. The game was actually a religious ritual to the Native American Indians.[15]

The English traders traveled over existing Indian trails. They brought shirts, hats, shoes, blankets, mirrors, ribbons, jewelry, pipes and tobacco, dolls, and other toys. They also supplied hatchets, tomahawks, knives, guns, ammunition, scissors, needles, pots, and kettles on the backs of many packhorses. Most Indian traders built log cabins to live and trade in.

How would your life change if new tools, toys and technology that you never had before were suddenly available?

John Frazier, George Croghan, William Trent, Alexander McKee, and James O'Hara were some of the first traders in early Pittsburgh.

Many of the Indian Traders learned to speak native American languages to negotiate buying land and making treaties between the Indians and white settlers. The Indians didn't understand the idea of a single person owning land.[16] They thought of the land as a range for their hunting instead of a piece of ground to take for your own and grow crops. Owning land made no more sense to the Indians than saying that you could own a piece of air or sunlight. Even Indian chiefs couldn't sell land since the Indians land was communal, meaning that it was all of theirs to use, not own.[17]

Why did the Indians think that owning land was as ridiculous as owning a piece of air or sunlight?

When the Indians saw forts being built, they at first thought that these were just to help with the trading posts. They didn't understand that the soldiers were there to protect the settlers who came to take their land and make this into their own farms. They didn't know at first that these settlers would force the Indians to move away.

Unfortunately, some Indian traders were dishonest and took advantage of the Indians by cheating them in many ways. The Indians became angry with white people because of this. They became even angrier when they realized that the white people were taking away their hunting grounds. The colonial governors tried to keep the white settlers from moving into Indian hunting ground, but they were unable to keep them out. In fact, some of the British officials were getting rich by obtaining large pieces of Indian land as land grants and then selling it to settlers.[18] For that reason the Indians began to choose white allies who were less harmful to their life style. First they sided with the French instead of the English.

If you were a Native American what would you think of the Europeans moving into your neighborhood?

The French fur traders were there mostly to buy furs and were not interested in staying to farm the land.[19] After the Revolutionary War ended, the Indians sided with the English instead of the Americans.[20]

They still hoped that the English would help them keep the Americans from moving further west to settle.

George Washington

Governor Robert Dinwiddie, Governor of Virginia, recognized how important it would be to have an English fort at the Forks of the Ohio, where the Allegheny and Monongahela Rivers meet. Whoever controlled that site (which would become Pittsburgh) would also control passage down the Ohio River, to the Mississippi River, all the way to New Orleans. In 1753, he decided to send a letter to the French Commander demanding that the French withdraw from land that he believed to be part of Virginia. George Washington, a tall young man in the Virginia Militia, volunteered for the job. Christopher Gist and the Indian Chief Guyasuta guided George Washington to the nearest French fort, Fort Le Boeuf. The French were polite, but sent him away, saying that they would give the letter to their commander in New France (Canada), and would only follow his orders.

Washington and his guide, Christopher Gist (a famous frontier scout who lived near Uniontown), narrowly escaped death on the way back to Virginia. They had reached the north bank of the partially frozen Allegheny River in late December. Across the river lay the Delaware Indian village called Shannopin's Town (near present-day Lawrenceville).[21] It took them all day to build a raft

Vocabulary Words

raft   hatchet   debris

and it was dark when they tried to cross the river. The raft was caught-up in blocks of ice and the men were thrown into the icy waters. Fortunately, they were near an island in the river called Wainwright's Island, which they reached safely and stayed there overnight.[22] The rivers change with flooding and the amount of debris that is swept along with the spring thaw every year. The island that George and Christopher stayed on is no longer there. The exact location of this crossing is unknown, but the 40th Street Bridge that crosses the Allegheny River in Lawrenceville today is also called "Washington's Crossing."

On the Monongahela River where it meets the Youghiogheny River lived a group of Seneca Indians ruled by Queen Aliquippa. George Washington visited Queen Aliquippa on his first trip through Pittsburgh in 1753. She became a close ally of Washington and refused to even meet with the French. Queen Aliquippa, her son, and her people went to Great Meadows to witness the battle of Fort Necessity. The French Indian Allies were against her because she was a friend to the English. After Washington's defeat at Fort Necessity, Queen Aliquippa fled to Aughwick, George Croghan's home, staying till she died on December 23, 1754.[23]

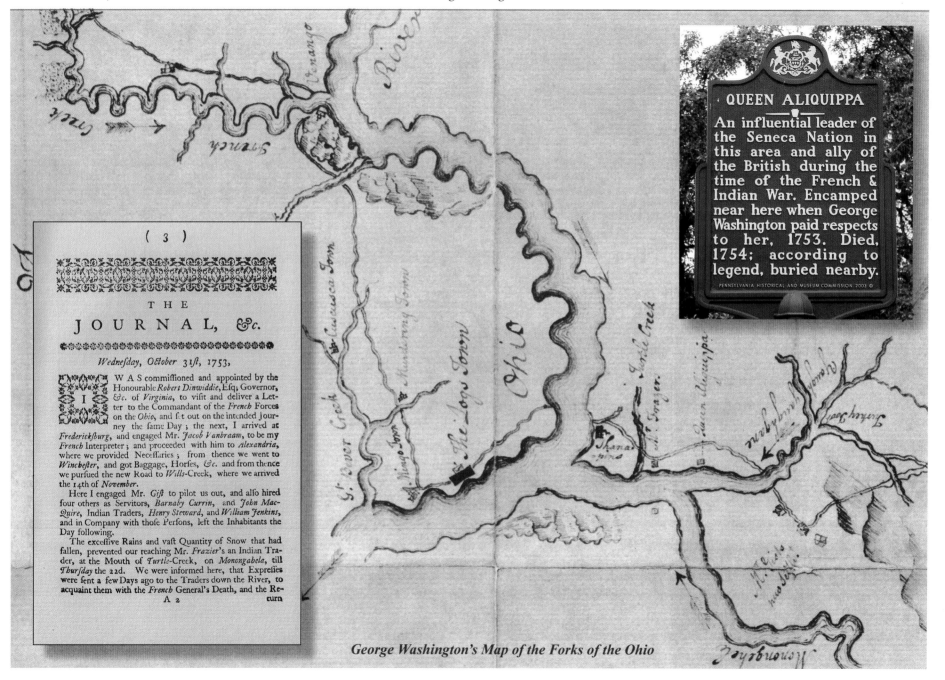

QUEEN ALIQUIPPA

An influential leader of the Seneca Nation in this area and ally of the British during the time of the French & Indian War. Encamped near here when George Washington paid respects to her, 1753. Died, 1754; according to legend, buried nearby.

PENNSYLVANIA HISTORICAL AND MUSEUM COMMISSION 2003 ©

(3)

THE

JOURNAL, &c.

Wednesday, October 31st, 1753,

I WAS commissioned and appointed by the Honourable *Robert Dinwiddie*, Esq; Governor, &c. of *Virginia*, to visit and deliver a Letter to the Commandant of the *French* Forces on the *Ohio*, and set out on the intended journey the same Day ; the next, I arrived at *Fredericksburg*, and engaged Mr. *Jacob Vanbraam*, to be my *French* Interpreter ; and proceeded with him to *Alexandria*, where we provided Necessaries ; from thence we went to *Winchester*, and got Baggage, Horses, &c. and from thence we pursued the new Road to *Wills*-Creek, where we arrived the 14th of *November*.

Here I engaged Mr. *Gist* to pilot us out, and also hired four others as Servitors, *Barnaby Currin*, and *John Mac-Quire*, Indian Traders, *Henry Steward*, and *William Jenkins*, and in Company with those Persons, left the Inhabitants the Day following.

The excessive Rains and vast Quantity of Snow that had fallen, prevented our reaching Mr. *Frazier*'s an Indian Trader, at the Mouth of *Turtle*-Creek, on *Monongahela*, till *Thursday* the 22d. We were informed here, that Expresses were sent a few Days ago to the Traders down the River, to acquaint them with the *French* General's Death, and the Re-

A 2   turn

George Washington's Map of the Forks of the Ohio

9

Land Speculators

Vocabulary Words

survey

surveyor

Mason-Dixon Line

petition

land speculation

proprietor

The image of a surveyor in this illustration is based on a life-like model of a surveyor that is on exhibit at the Fort Pitt Museum in Pittsburgh, Pennsylvania. The museum is located on the ground at the Forks of the Ohio (now called the Point) where Fort Pitt stood. Near the museum building stands the Fort Pitt Block House. It is the only building still remaining of the original Fort.

On his trip to deliver the warning letter to the French at Fort Le Boeuf, George Washington stayed at John Frazier's trading post near the Monongahela River.

There, in his journal, he wrote:

"As I got down before the canoe,
I spent some time viewing the rivers,
and the land in the Fork; which
I think extremely well situated for a Fort,
as it has the absolute command of both
rivers. The land at the point is 20 or 25
feet above the common surface of the
water, and it is considerable bottom of
flat, well-timbered land all around it,
very convenient for building."

Standing at the forks of the Ohio, young George saw forest stretching as far as he could see, with the three rivers joining together in the middle. Washington's report was very popular both in Williamsburg and England. The English were determined to build a fort on the land in the fork of those three rivers. The Native American Indians had named the three rivers that met there, at "the forks." Delawares named *"Allegewi,"* ("Allegheny") the "river in the land in which they came from distant parts." They also used *"Monongahela,"* to mean "high falling in banks." The Senecas used the word *"Ohio"* to mean "beautiful river."[24]

Various people formed many land companies in the east that petitioned the King of England and the British Parliament for grants of land. The King of England made William Penn the proprietor of Pennsylvania. Penn paid the Indians for parcels of Pennsylvania lands at various times. Governor Dinwiddie along with George Washington's half brothers and others were investors in the Ohio Land Company.[25] Virginia included the entire Monongahela Valley in its land system. The Ohio Land Company sent surveyors to make maps. They also sent Christopher Gist to explore the land and establish relationships with the Indians for trading. George Croghan, called "the King of the Indian Traders," was also a land speculator.

Croghan traveled back and forth across Pennsylvania and was asked for advice by the Philadelphia Assembly on how to protect the Frontier. He suggested a series of forts across Pennsylvania to what would become Pittsburgh.[26] These he thought would give protection to the settlers when the Indians sometimes attacked them. There were many more land speculators from the various American Colonies. There were land companies that used advertisements to describe western lands in glorious terms without including a description of the hardships of travel and pioneer life. Some people were not able to endure the rough pioneer life in the west. They gave up their dream and went back east to live.

Both Virginia and Pennsylvania claimed the land in western Pennsylvania. Since there wasn't an accurate map, there wasn't an established boundary between the two colonies. The boundary dispute between Pennsylvania and Virginia didn't end until August 31, 1779.[27] Then they agreed to extend the Mason Dixon Line due west 5 degrees computed from the Delaware River (creating the southern straight edge of Western Pennsylvania). From there they made a meridian (a north to south line) drawn to the north limit of the state (up to Lake Erie) to create the western straight edge.[28]

Forts at the Forks of the Ohio

Red text represents English actions and decisions.

Blue text represents French actions and decisions.

Black text represents Philadelphia Assembly actions and decisions.

Vocabulary Words

French and Indian War

Fort Necessity

retreat

army regulars

reveille

ally

allies

Quakers

pacifist

After George Washington's Journal was printed, he was ordered to return to the Forks of the Ohio to check on the progress of "Fort Prince George" being built there by a former Indian trader, Captain William Trent. When the French learned about this English fort, they sent a large force of about 500 soldiers with cannons down the Allegheny River from Canada. There were only 41 English soldiers at Fort Prince George when the French arrived. The English were forced to retreat to Virginia. Colonel Joshua Fry and George Washington marched to the forks to rebuild Fort Prince George. Before arriving at the Forks of the Ohio, they learned that the French had already built Fort Duquesne in its place. About 25 miles east of the forks, Washington and his soldiers attacked a group of French soldiers, killing a dozen and taking the rest prisoner. It was the beginning of the French and Indian War.

When the French at Fort Duquesne learned of this attack, they set out to find Washington's group. When Washington learned of the French military movement, he retreated to an area known as the Great Meadows near the Youghiogheny River. He had his men quickly build a fort to defend themselves against the

French. He called it "Fort Necessity." Washington chose this site for a Fort because he believed that the French would fight in the traditional European style in the open Meadow.

The French and their Indian allies numbered over 600 and by the time Washington reached the Great Meadows he only had about 300 soldiers left. Instead of fighting in the open, the French and Indians attacked, using the cover of the surrounding forest, shooting down on the fort from the surrounding hills.

George Washington and his men fought the French during a steady rain, all day, on July 3, 1754, until 8:00 o'clock at night. By then one third of his army was dead or wounded. Rain had made their gunpowder useless. Then the French offered to discuss terms of surrender. Outnumbered and with no hope of winning, Washington had to accept. He and his men surrendered and retreated to Virginia.[29]

The next year Major General Edward Braddock was appointed commander of English forces in America. He had been a soldier for 45 years and was used to fighting in Europe. In February, 1755, Braddock chose to lead the expedition himself against Fort Duquesne. George Washington, was one of General Braddock's officers, who helped to prepare the army. There were no roads to Fort Duquesne, so General Braddock had his soldiers cut their own road, which was only 12 feet wide, across the mountains and through the dense forest. General Braddock only knew how to fight in the European way. His army came with music, banners, mounted officers, redcoat regulars, and blue coat Virginians, wagons, cannons, cattle, axe men and bridge builders. They had to stop to make bridges over streams.

The French soon learned that the English army was approaching Fort Duquesne. They could easily hear the English coming. They sent 250 French and 600 Indians to stop them, including an Indian named Pontiac. A battle took place near the Monongahela River, at an area that became known as "Braddock's Field," where the town of Braddock, Pennsylvania is located today. The French and Indians fought the Indian way of fighting by staying behind trees, rocks, and bushes while the English continued to march and stay on the road. The English were surrounded and forced to retreat.

456 soldiers were killed and 421 were wounded, and General Braddock himself died from wounds four days later at Christopher Gist's farm.

Thomas Penn supported the idea of a fort on the Ohio River to protect Pennsylvania from the French and their Indian allies. The Philadelphia Assembly controlled the political power in Pennsylvania. Many of the Assembly were Quakers and were pacifists. They didn't believe in killing or providing money for armies of men with guns to protect the settlers. They also refused to arm the Indians. Instead, they wanted to win the good will of the Indians by giving gifts to them.[30] This plan worked for a while, but as more settlers migrated to the west to make farms, the Indian tribes refused to give up their lands. They started attacking and killing the settlers. The news of Braddock's defeat reached Philadelphia at the same time that Indians began attacking and killing settlers closer to that city. When these attacks continued, the Pennsylvania Assembly finally allowed money to be spent on sending ammunition and soldiers to defend the Frontier.

In 1758, William Pitt, the prime minister of England, gave the English General John Forbes the job of capturing Fort Duquesne. His army included 2,000 regulars, 2,500 men from Pennsylvania, 1,500 men from Virginia and 1,000 from other colonies. Over the protests of George Washington, General Forbes decided to build a large road over the mountains to take his army to Fort Duquesne. George Washington wanted the road to come through Virginia. General Forbes could have followed the narrow trail used by General Braddock, that went through Virginia, but decided instead to make a larger more permanent road from Philadelphia to the Forks of the Ohio. That meant that General Forbes' army spent most of the summer and fall building the road over the Pennsylvania mountains to reach Bedford by September. One of Forbes' officers, Major James Grant, was anxious to show his superior military ability. He considered the colonial soldiers as primitive and incapable. He persuaded General Forbes to let him go ahead to Fort Duquesne with 800 Highlander soldiers (Scottish soldiers that wore kilts) to test the French strength. On September 13th he reached the hill above Fort Duquesne (that became known as "Grant's Hill"). The next morning he had his drummers beat the reveille to scare the French. Instead of being scared by this, the French and Indians came out and attacked. They killed or captured one third of Grant's

13

men. Grant himself was captured. Apparently this experience did not make Grant humble or less convinced of his own abilities. After being ransomed, Grant blamed the colonial soldiers for his disaster.[31]

By November, the rest of the English army had traveled as far as Fort Ligonier, about 30 miles east of the forks. George Washington wrote that only a miracle could bring this expedition to a happy ending. But luck was changing for the English. The Delaware and Shawnee Indians had become friends with the English instead of the French. Fort Duquesne was not very large and was beginning to fall apart.

The French realized that Fort Duquesne was too small and did not have enough soldiers or cannon to resist the large English army. With low food provisions, the French were also unable to feed their Indian allies and sent most of them home. Only a few hundred French remained. The French decided to abandon Fort Duquesne.

When General Forbes and George Washington reached the the forks on November 25th, they found Fort Duquesne had been burned to ashes, and the French had fled. On November 27, 1758, General Forbes wrote a letter to William Pitt, telling him that he had named the town located at the Forks of the Ohio, "Pittsbourgh" and was building a new fort there to be named "Fort Pitt".

How Pioneers Traveled to Pittsburgh

Vocabulary Words

pack horse

squatter

settler

ferry

flatboat

cargo

tomahawk

dry goods

hardware

John was afraid to ask his Father, but he really wanted to know how much longer it would be before they got there. That is, to Pittsburgh. They had been walking for six weeks now with their pack horses, their animals, and the other families. John's younger sister, Margaret, and younger brother, Henry, were too young to walk much, so they sat in a hickory basket tied onto one of the pack horses. There were chickens in a crate tied onto another pack horse. John's mother, Sarah, walked beside the lead pack horse. John's job was to lead the cows along. He had enjoyed the adventure at first, seeing land he had never looked at before. But he soon learned that it was easier coming down the mountains than climbing up them. The forest was so thick with trees that the path they were on could just allow the horses and animals to walk along in single file. They couldn't have used a wagon to carry everything that they wanted to bring to start a new home. John saw his Father excitingly motioning at the top of the hill. They hurried up as fast as they could to meet him. Then they saw what had made his Father so enthusiastic. There, before them, they looked down on the little village of Pittsburgh. Fort Pitt was bigger than they had even imagined. Outside of the Fort there were log houses, about five of them were stores. John and his family would join the camp of people on the side of the Monongahela. They would wait there for their flatboat to be built and for the water in the rivers to rise high enough from the spring thaw. Then they would load their animals, belongings, and themselves onto the boat and float down the Ohio River into the West.

Before the Revolutionary War some settlers came west and for protection tried to make farms close to the forts. They often had to flee inside of the forts when Indians raided and attacked. Many became discouraged and moved back east. During the Revolutionary War, no new settlers came west. After the war, Indian treaties made in 1784 and 1785 allowed land to be bought at 30 pounds for 100 acres. Many settlers came after the War who didn't buy or receive permission to come from anyone. They cleared trees and built cabins and were known as squatters. Earlier pioneers had marked off land that they wanted to come back and settle on but couldn't stay there to live until it was safe to return. They used a tomahawk to mark trees around the area they called their own and carved their initials and sometimes their name on these. This was called "Tomahawk Rights."[32] When they returned, sometimes their claims were allowed, but often other settlers had already built a cabin and started to farm there, or the land had been bought by another.[33]

Many Indian trails crossed Pennsylvania from east to west. They usually followed streams and rivers or along ridges of mountains. The Frankstown Path was known as a main road. The eastern part of it is now part of the Wil-

liam Penn Highway. The western section of the Frankstown Path followed the Kittanning Path, that connected Frankstown to Kittanning. Along the Raystown Path the Pennsylvania Road was built. Part of the Raystown Path became part of the Lincoln Highway. Most of the Nemacolin's Path from Cumberland, Maryland, to Brownsville and then to

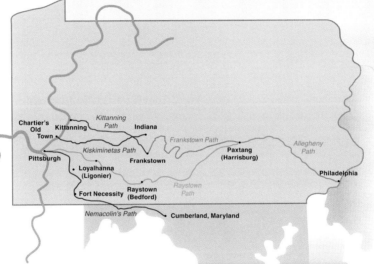

Pittsburgh, was used by General Braddock to build his road. The Kiskiminetas Path passed from Indiana to Tarentum (Chartier's Old Town).[34] The Allegheny Path connected Philadelphia to Paxtang (Harrisburg).

The poorest pioneers simply walked across Pennsylvania carrying their belongings on their back.

How long would it take you to walk across Pennsylvania?

Those who could afford it went by pack horses.[35] A family used several pack horses. On these they carried the youngest children sitting in baskets, inbetween tied-on crates. Babies, chickens, and little pigs were also carried in tied-on baskets. Farm tools, food supplies, tents and bedding, clothes, dishes, and kitchenware were all tied-onto the pack horses. They also drove their animals (the cows, cattle, sheep, and hogs) along with them.[36] The men and boys drove the animals and scouted out the path ahead.

How long would it take you to walk to school from your home?

Commercial pack horse trains were also used to carry cargo between east and west. A man rode on the first horse, and another man on the last horse in the train. Each horse's reins inbetween these horses were tied to the horse in front of him. The pack horse trains going west carried things the pioneers couldn't make themselves including salt, dry goods, and hardware.

What would you want to take on your packhorse to your new home?

The trains traveling east carried furs, whiskey, and ginseng (an American herb used to make medicine).

Conestoga Freight Wagons

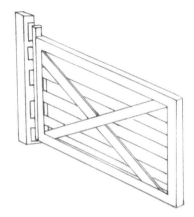

Vocabulary Words

Conestoga Wagon

stage coach

hames

fee

maintenance

teamster

cargo

General Braddock and General Forbes made the first roads across Virginia, Maryland and Pennsylvania to take their armies, guns, and supplies with them to the Forks of the Ohio. They fought to capture the French Fort Duquesne and then build the English Fort Pitt. Wagons were not used much for crossing Pennsylvania until after 1790, when the first roads were improved.[37]

The primary way to transport freight or cargo over Pennsylvania's early roads was in a Conestoga wagon.[38] These wagons were first made in the Conestoga Valley near Lancaster, Pennsylvania. These wagons were called "Turnpike Schooners." They looked like schooner sail ships traveling along the roads. Special large and strong horses were bred to pull them. Usually, six horses pulled about six tons of freight for up to 14 miles a day.

The men who drove Conestoga wagons were known as "teamsters" because they drove a "team" of horses. They were rugged outdoors men who gave some new words and phrases to the English language. The word "teamster" still refers to people who haul freight, now by trucks. The early teamsters often smoked short cigars that became known as "stogies" (after Cone"STOGA").[39] They wore high boots held together with square wooden pegs driven through round leather holes. ("You can't put a square peg in a round hole," is a phrase that came from this.) When the Conestoga drivers stopped at Inns along their route, the bartenders recorded how much they owed him by marking "P's" and "Q's" on a chalkboard ("P" for pints, and "Q" for quarts). "Mind your P's and Q's," is a phrase that came from this practice and means to be careful of your actions.[40]

17

The Conestoga wagon body was about 24 feet long and sagged in the middle so that the freight inside would slide to the middle and not out the ends when the wagon went up and over bumps in the road. The lower part of the bed was painted blue, and the upper sides painted red. White cloth covered the curving wooden bows and was tied closed in the front and back to protect the cargo from weather and dust. A toolbox hung from the rear and ornate iron reinforcements held the sides and ends together. Wagoner bells were hung on an iron bow above the horse's hames (similar in sound to later use of sleigh bells). These Conestoga wagons had no passenger

seats. Instead the driver could walk beside the lead horse (first on the left side), or ride on the wheel horse (third on the left side, closest to the wagon wheel), or pull out and sit on the swivel board, called the lazy board, on the left side of the wagon. Cars and trucks today are driven by a steering wheel positioned on the left side of the vehicle because of the custom of steering a horse wagon from the left side.[41] To steer the wagon the driver held a long line attached to the lead horse. He would call out "gee" to tell the horses to turn right, or "haw" to tell the horses to turn left.

These Conestoga freight wagons traveled mostly between Philadelphia, Pittsburgh, and Baltimore. Sometimes two to three pioneer families hired one of these wagons to carry their belongings across the mountains to Pittsburgh. Sometimes members of the family traveled behind the wagons carrying their things, driving herds of their animals with them. These Conestoga wagons were much larger than the "Prairie Schooners" that the pioneers would later use further west to cross the plains of the United States.

The improved roads had pikes (or gates) along them that required travelers to stop and pay a fee there for use of the road. Then the pikes were turned to the side so the wagon could proceed. This road then became known as the "turnpike." Stagecoaches began to be used to carry passengers and mail over Pennsylvania roads. They were the most "comfortable" and fastest way to travel, and they stopped at the better inns at night to rest. Usually women and children slept in the inn's bedrooms with several people in the same bed. The men slept on the floor of the large dining room. Food was often good at the better inns, but travelers complained that even the best inns had fleas in the beds.

To keep stagecoaches from falling over sideways, often the travelers had to help by leaning to one side and then to the other side when the coaches swayed in the road ruts. Sometimes the passengers had to get out and help push the wagons out of muddy ruts.

Can you imagine having to get out and help push the stagecoach out of the mud along the way?

Taverns, inns, towns, and villages were started all along the pioneer trails between the eastern towns and Pittsburgh. Some of these towns became popular places to visit. The number of packhorse drivers, Conestoga teamsters and pioneers traveling along the Pennsylvania roads increased greatly. In the center of many towns there was a square area called the "Diamond." This Diamond was where the Conestoga horses could rest for the night.[42] There were taverns around the square where people could eat and sleep. In Pittsburgh, this original square was located at the intersection of Market and Diamond Streets. The early food market located there was called the "Diamond Market."

Do you have grandparents who can remember the Diamond Market in downtown Pittsburgh? Do you know how Market Square and other streets and places got their names?

Fort Pitt Saves the Town of Pittsburgh

Legend

Commandant's House

A   Ditch
B   Guard Room
C   Drawbridge
D   Soldier Barracks
E   Officer Barracks
F   Well
G   Block House

Vocabulary Words

rampart

bastion

pentagon

small pox

Fort Pitt was finished being built in 1761 by General John Stanwix. It covered 17 and ½ acres and was a much larger, stronger fort than Fort Duquesne had been.[43] Fort Duquesne was near the fountain at today's Point. Fort Pitt was built further inland and on high ground, away from the Point. Fort Pitt was the strongest, most elaborate fort in British North America at that time. The sides of Fort Pitt were not just wooden. It had large earth sides that could not be broken or burned by cannon balls or flaming arrows. Fort Pitt was shaped like a pentagon with five sides and bastions at each of the five corners where soldiers could defend the Fort.

A large ditch surrounded it.[44]

Fort Pitt's walls (ramparts) and bastions were 20 feet high by 60 feet wide and were made of earth. On the land sides the walls were line with brick. Sod was attached the walls on the river sides.[45] It took a great amount of physical effort to build Fort Pitt. Fort Pitt was constructed completely by hand, using picks, shovels, and wheelbarrows.[46]

How long would it take you to build a large fort, like Fort Pitt, using only hand tools?

More settlers began coming to Pittsburgh after Fort Pitt was built. In 1761, there were about 300 people living outside the fort. The Indians often came to the fort to trade furs for food. In native culture people shared their food. They assumed the English would share. The English settlers didn't understand the way the Indians lived. They thought that they were lazy for not cutting down trees and growing crops. The Indians didn't understand the English settlers. They couldn't understand why anyone would take the land to use only for him or herself. When the Indians realized that the settlers were taking away their hunting grounds and trying to make them move away they became angry.[47]

In 1763, an Indian chief named Pontiac organized the Indians to fight the settlers and to attack all the forts. The Indian leader who attacked Fort Pitt was Chief Guyasuta,[48] who had previously been a guide for George Washington. Some Indians remained friendly, but others attacked settlers while they worked in their fields and houses. Guyasuta wanted peace, but he realized that he had to protect his people, so he tried to make the English go back East.

How would you feel if new people moved into your city and wanted to change the way you lived?

Captain Simeon Ecuyer, the Commander at Fort Pitt, knew that the Indians were going to attack, so he ordered the settlers around the fort to come inside. He prepared the Fort for a long siege by storing immense amounts

of food, water, and animals. He then had the settler's cabins outside the fort torn down or burned so that the Indians could not use them for shelter or protection when they attacked Fort Pitt.[49] He used the wood from these cabins to build temporary shelters between the barracks and the rampart walls of Fort Pitt for the settlers to live in. Fort Pitt had three wells for water. Captain Ecuyer placed barrels of water around the fort to use in case of fire, and assigned the women in the fort the duties of "fire-lassies" in case a large fire occurred.[50] Captain Ecuyer also had a small hand fire pump, called a "water engine," [51] in the Fort that proved to be valuable.[52] Captain Ecuyer asked English General Amherst for reinforcements. General Amherst sent Colonel Bouquet with a small force to aide Fort Pitt. Meanwhile, the Indians tried to talk the English into leaving Fort Pitt. The Indians there said that they were trying to keep other Indians who were attacking Fort Ligonier from attacking Fort Pitt. They also said that they would let the English travel back east

Defending Fort Pitt.

Instead of fighting a large battle, the Indians made small, cotinuous attacks with rifles and arrows throughout the Summer of 1763. The Indians shot fire arrows into the fort damaging some buildings. The women in the fort made a bucket brigade and put out the flames.

and not hurt them if they left.[53] Indians had made this same promise before, but instead of helping, they had attacked the English soldiers and settlers when they came out of their forts. This time the English told the Indians that a large army of soldiers was coming to help them. The soldiers then sent the Indians away with blankets from the small pox hospital in the fort.

Why were small pox blankets given to the Indians?

Then, the Indians did attack Fort Pitt. The Indians shot fire arrows into the fort setting some buildings on fire. The women in the fort made a bucket brigade and put out the flames.[54] Realizing that they could not break into Fort Pitt, the same group of Indians decided to try to stop Colonel Bouquet from reaching the Fort.

On his way to Fort Pitt, Colonel Bouquet rested his army at Fort Ligonier for two days, and then led his troops towards Pittsburgh. He came to a place called Bushy Run, 25 miles east of Pittsburgh. There he was surrounded by the large group of Indians who had previously attacked Fort Pitt. After two days of fighting his soldiers were running out of water. He decided to pretend that his army was retreating. He secretly sent some of the men around the outside of the Indian location. When the Indians attacked what they thought was a retreat, the English surrounded the Indians and defeated them. The Indians were surprised that the English soldiers had

learned to fight like this. They realized that they couldn't stop these English from holding onto land near Fort Pitt, so they decided to move further west instead of continuing to fight at Fort Pitt.[55] Although Indians continued to fight the settlers in other places, this was the last time that Fort Pitt was attacked by Indians.

In Point Park today there is one building, still standing, that was part of Fort Pitt – the Block House. The configuration and use of the Block House changed many times. It was even used as a residence. James O'Hara, a former Indian trader, bought the land that Fort Pitt's Block House was built on. In 1895, his granddaughter, Mary Schenley, gave the Block House and land to the Fort Pitt Society of the Daughters of the American Revolution. She also donated land for a park, which is known as Schenley Park.[56]

The Pioneer Town of Pittsburgh

The houses in Pittsburgh didn't have numbers at first. Taverns and stores were known by their owners and had colorful signs with pictures hung outside to identify them.[57] Sometimes the signs were funny. One of them, the "Whale and the Monkey" read "Here the weary may rest, the hungry feed, and those who thirst may quaff the best."

Some of the other Tavern signs included:

The Three Bells

The Green Tree

The Black Bear

The Golden Cross Keys

Sign of the Buck

The Black Horse

The Red Lion

Vocabulary Words

orderly grid

parallel

cooper

tanner & currier

blacksmith

whitesmith

tinner

malster & brewer

wheelwright

The Pioneer village of Pittsburgh grew quickly. In 1769, William Penn's sons opened a land office in Pittsburgh. They quickly had thousands of applications for 300-acre farms.[58] In 1784, Colonel George Woods was hired by the Penn family to lay out the street plans for the triangle-shaped town of Pittsburgh. His street plan started at the fort and included all the land up to Grant's Hill (the area known today as Grant Street). Throughout the town were several ponds. The largest was Hogg's Pond, which is where Macy's Department Store is now located. Dirt taken from Grant's Hill was used to fill in the pond so buildings could be built there.

Besides ponds, there were log houses with plots of land surrounding them. Colonel Woods proposed widening the lanes between those log houses into larger streets. The settlers in those houses objected strongly to changing their properties. They were afraid that their property value would decrease with these changes. For this reason, instead of establishing an orderly grid of streets of the same size, Colonel Woods left the settler's buildings and lots where they were and laid out streets between them with different widths to accommodate the existing properties.[59] Even today, there are narrow streets of varying widths in the triangle section of downtown Pittsburgh. Mr. Woods did add Liberty and Penn Streets (now Avenues) to run parallel to the Allegheny River through what had been the garden of Fort Pitt. He also

created a market square called the Diamond (now called Market Square).

By 1792 in Pittsburgh, there were:

1 clock and watchmaker

2 coopers (barrel makers)

1 skin dresser and breeches maker (made buckskin and cow hide clothing)

2 tanners and curriers (made animal hides into leather)

4 cabinetmakers

2 hatters

2 weavers

5 blacksmiths

5 shoemakers

3 saddlers

1 malster and brewer (The Point Brewery)

2 tinners (made tin cups, plates, kitchen tools, candle holders, lanterns, etc.)

3 wheelwrights (wagon wheels)

1 stocking weaver

1 rope maker

2 whitesmiths (people who finished and polished iron and tin pieces)

Although the work being done was progressive, the town of Pittsburgh was still a rough looking place. In 1789, a visitor called Pittsburgh the muddiest place he had ever seen. There were no sidewalks. No streets were paved. A few owners had put wooden planks in front of their houses and shops but most hadn't. The streets were described as "filled with hogs, dogs, horse carts and noisy children." There were no streetlights at night. A lamp was hung over the doors of taverns and inns, but everywhere else in town it was very dark.[60]

Gateway to the West

Treaty of Greenville in 1795 – This Treaty, between the United States government and the Six Nations of native Americans, ended some of the hostilities that prevented many pioneers from trying to move beyond the frontier town of Pittsburgh.

Vocabulary Words

spring thaw

debris

sand bar

navigate

chaff

Some of the pioneers who came to Pittsburgh had no desire to move further west. But after the Greenville Treaty in 1795,* it was then possible to safely continue west to find fertile land for farming. However, there were no roads to the west from Pittsburgh. There were no railroads either. The pioneers who intended to travel beyond Pittsburgh had only one way to get there. It was the Ohio River.

How would you get around if there were no roads to travel on?

And on that river, the flatboat was the cheapest and most convenient transportation for the pioneer. Those pioneers who had driven their wagons over the frozen mountains to Pittsburgh camped near the river while their flatboats were being built. Those who already had bought their flatboats were able to camp inside of them. Using the stove in the flatboat, they kept warmer than those who had to sleep in tents or in their wagons.[61] The pioneers had to wait for the spring thaw when the frozen rivers began to break-up enough to allow their boats through the icy waters. This thawing meant that the level of water in the rivers would rise high enough so that there were fewer shallow areas for the boats to navigate. Submerged tree trunks, sand bars, and rocks were hidden dangers in the rivers. Every year after the spring thaw, the underwater hazards of the rivers changed because of the debris that had been swept into the rivers during storms.

What would be fun about traveling down the Ohio River in a flatboat with your family and farm animals?

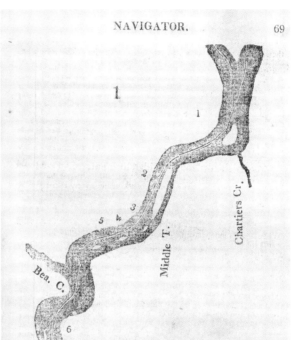

This is a map, from the 1818 Edition of The Navigator, showing the important features of the Ohio River from Pittsburgh to the town of Beaver, about 3/4 of a mile below the Big Beaver Creek.

Zadok Cramer recognized there was a need for immigrants to know how to travel down the Ohio River. And so, he wrote and published a book titled *The Navigator* in 1801. He updated it through 12 editions until 1824.

a bow saw

a wood plane

a chaffing fork

an auger

Sharon and Anna listened to Uncle Robert play his fiddle. It made shelling the corn easier as they all camped beside the river, waiting for the spring thaw.

a pick

Some of the tools the pioneers used.

Zadok Cramer

Vocabulary Words

bookbinder

publisher

almanack

territory

caulk

Zadok Cramer, a bookbinder and publisher, came to Pittsburgh in 1800.[62] He bought John Gilkinson's bookstore. He offered his bookbinding skills and his ability to make blank books and he had printed books to sell. He hung out the "Sign of the Franklin Head," using Benjamin Franklin as his advertisement. He wrote and printed *The Navigator* and also published a yearly *Almanack*.

Why do you think that Zadok Cramer used Benjamin Franklin as his advertisement?

Shortly after President Jefferson's inauguration, Cramer published a best-selling book describing the difficult political struggle that happened during Jefferson's election.

When Cramer first published *The Navigator*, France still owned the vast area of land on the western side of the Mississippi River known as the Louisiana Territory. After President Jefferson purchased this territory for America, the number of immigrants migrating to the west increased greatly, as did the sales of *The Navigator*. President Jefferson hired Meriwether Lewis and William Clark to explore and to make maps of this new part of America. After their famous adventure, Cramer published *The Journal of Patrick Gass*, an account of the Lewis and Clark adventure written by Patrick Gass, who was a member of the Lewis and Clark expedition.

All along the Monongahela River, flatboats were being built. The cost of a flatboat was from $1 to $1.50 per foot of length. The first flatboats were very plain. On one end they had a cabin to protect the family and

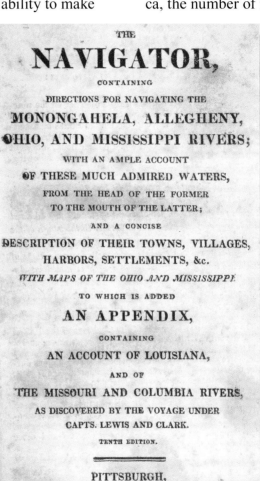

THE

NAVIGATOR,

CONTAINING

DIRECTIONS FOR NAVIGATING THE

MONONGAHELA, ALLEGHENY, OHIO, AND MISSISSIPPI RIVERS;

WITH AN AMPLE ACCOUNT

OF THESE MUCH ADMIRED WATERS,

FROM THE HEAD OF THE FORMER
TO THE MOUTH OF THE LATTER;

AND A CONCISE

DESCRIPTION OF THEIR TOWNS, VILLAGES, HARBORS, SETTLEMENTS, &c.

WITH MAPS OF THE OHIO AND MISSISSIPPI

TO WHICH IS ADDED

AN APPENDIX,

CONTAINING

AN ACCOUNT OF LOUISIANA,

AND OF

THE MISSOURI AND COLUMBIA RIVERS,

AS DISCOVERED BY THE VOYAGE UNDER
CAPTS. LEWIS AND CLARK.

TENTH EDITION.

PITTSBURGH,

PRINTED AND PUBLISHED BY CRAMER & SPEAR,

FRANKLIN HEAD, WOOD STREET.

1818.

their belongings. They also needed to be big enough to hold the animals on the opposite end. These boats had to be steered by oars (one on each side and one in the back) and by long poles. Flatboats could be very different in size depending upon the needs of the families using them. They included everything that could float from small boats to large barges. Those that were used for short trips were called "Kentucky boats" or "broadhorns."[63] Larger ones, used for long trips all the way down the Ohio and then down the Mississippi Rivers, were called "New Orleans boats." These were made much stronger than the Kentucky boats and were covered their whole length. They had slits in their wood sides for rifles to defend against Indians and Pirates that might attack them.

Zadok Cramer warned the Pioneers to check the caulking in between the planks of lumber on their boats. He also told them to take a friend with them when buying their flatboats.

How would you feel if the river water started to come into your boat between the wooden boards?

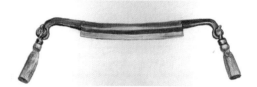

They needed someone who knew about boats, who could check for rotten wood and caulking that was poorly installed on the boat they expected to buy. He even told them to take along their own caulking to make repairs along the way if needed.[64] These flatboats were hard to steer and could not be taken back upstream against the current of the Ohio River. When the pioneers reached their destinations in their "Kentucky boats," they usually took the boats apart to reuse the wood. The lumber was either sold to the river towns to make sidewalks and buildings, or the pioneers took it with them to their farms. There, they used the lumber from their flatboats to make houses, barns, and furniture.[65]

What would you do with the lumber from your boat when you finished your journey on the Ohio River?

A "drawknife" was used by carpenters and coopers to shape and trim wood.

a hand saw

27

Pittsburgh's First Newspaper

Vocabulary Words

hand printing press

foundry type

Postmaster

On July 29, 1786, John Scull and Joseph Hall printed the first newspaper in Pittsburgh, called the *Pittsburgh Gazette*. It took the two of them over 10 hours to print 700 copies on a hand printing press.[66] They used metal type for the headlines and for the smaller words. They also printed ads in their newspaper for rags. The newspapermen offered to buy rags so they could make their own paper because transporting paper supplies over the mountains from the East was very expensive. Before the *Pittsburgh Gazette* was printed, the news was delivered by people using Conestoga wagons, stage coaches, and pack horses that took 6 to 8 weeks to come from the east.

Hugh Henry Brackenridge, a lawyer who had graduated from Princeton, had brought the printing press, type, and Mr. Scull and Mr. Hall to Pittsburgh. Mr. Brackenridge had come to Pittsburgh in 1781. He loved the town and wrote a story for that first issue of the *Pittsburgh Gazette* saying how wonderful Pittsburgh was to live in. The *Gazette* was the only newspaper in western Pennsylvania for nine years.

What would be exciting about reading the news in Pittsburgh's first newspaper?

At that time, there were 36 log houses, one stone house, one wooden frame house, and five small stores in Pittsburgh. Mr. Brackenridge predicted that Pittsburgh would become a town of great manufacturing.[67] The sale of farms and plantations was a regular news item in the *Gazette*. The *Gazette* published ferryboat schedules. Because there were no bridges across the Rivers, ferries were made to cross both the Monongahela and the Allegheny Rivers.[68] Three main ferries along the Monongahela River were called the Upper Ferry, Middle Ferry, and Lower Ferry. James Robinson's Ferry was the main crossing for the Allegheny River.

With plenty of trees to use, boat building became an early major industry. Pittsburgh, Brownsville, and Elizabeth, Pennsylvania, advertised boat building facilities in this newspaper. Brick making began with General Stanwix, who used bricks to build Fort Pitt.[69] Brick making developed quickly here because of the great quantity of natural clays. The *Gazette* was the source of information about coal mining, glass manufacture, and many other businesses as they emerged. What is now called "Mount Washington" was at first called

"Coal Hill." There were large seams of coal that could be seen along the surface. Surface mining became an early trade.

In 1797, the first glassworks began.[70] It was very difficult to bring glass in pack horse trains from the east. The largest windows that could be brought on a pack horse without breaking, were small, about 6 inches wide. James O'Hara, a former Indian trader and Quarter-master General for the U.S. Army, and Isaac Craig, a former officer in the American Revolution, hired William Eichbaum, a German glass maker, to run their plant. They were able to make much larger glass windows. They made windows as large as 18 by 24 inches. The cost of the windows made in Pittsburgh was much cheaper than glass transported all the way from the East.

What would your house look like if you only had one or two small 6 inch windows in it?

This meant that houses began to become much brighter inside with windows letting daylight come in. Besides windows, glass makers made glass bottles, plates, and cups.

In 1787, John Scull became the first postmaster of Pittsburgh. He operated the first post office at his *Pittsburgh Gazette* store on the corner of Market and First Streets.[71]

In 1791, Samuel Slater opened the first cotton mill in Pittsburgh.[72] He hired nine children who were 7 to 12 years of age to work in his cotton mill. The *Pittsburgh Gazette* advertised for apprentices for various trades including watch and clock makers, hatters, rope-makers, shoemakers, coopers, and glassworks.

What would it be like to work in a cotton mill instead of going to school?

The ropemakers used a tool called a "wimble" for turning braids of cord into rope.

29

Children's Life in Early Pittsburgh

A hand-carved washboard

Near each log cabin there usually was a small vegetable garden called a "truck patch" that the women and children took care of while the men planted and tended the large field crops as well as hunted for meat. In that truck patch, the pioneers grew corn, pump-kins, watermelons, turnips, squash, beans, and cabbage. The larger crops in the fields were corn, wheat, rye, oats, barley, hay, peas,

flax, and tobacco. All the farming was done by hand using an axe, hoe, scythe, maddox, and wooden plows.[73] All children helped out with family chores, including taking care of the garden, the animals, taking care of the younger chil-dren, gathering firewood, tending the fire, and help-ing prepare the food.[74]

In the evening, the children often worked to shell the corn by the light of the fireplace.

Children also had to help with soap making and clothes washing.[75] Clothes washing took all day. To wash clothes, wood had to be gath-ered to heat water in a large iron wash pot. That water had to be carried from a stream.

After boiling, the clothes were scrubbed on a washboard then wrung out. Next, the clothes were rinsed in cold water, and the women and children wrung them and laid them out to dry over bushes, from tree limbs, or strung on a cord to dry.

How long would it take you to carry enough firewood and water to do the laundry?

Vocabulary Words

axe

hoe

scythe

maddox

wooden plow

shell corn

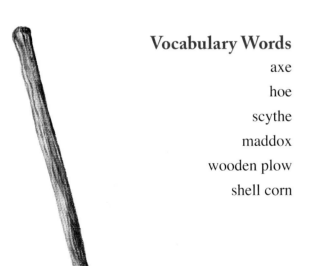

A maddox

The only soap they had was made from animal fat and lye. The ashes from fireplaces

a wooden hopper for making soap

were saved in a wooden ash hopper that had a slit in the bottom with straw along it to act like a strainer. When the hopper was full, women poured water over the ashes and the liquid that ran out was called lye. This was boiled until it became thick. Women saved fat from their cooking. The fatty oils were mixed with the lye and salt was added, then it was boiled. Soap rose to the surface of the liquid. The upper crust hardened and could be cut into bars, or chipped and flaked.

What do you think it would be like to use soap made out of lye and cooking fat?

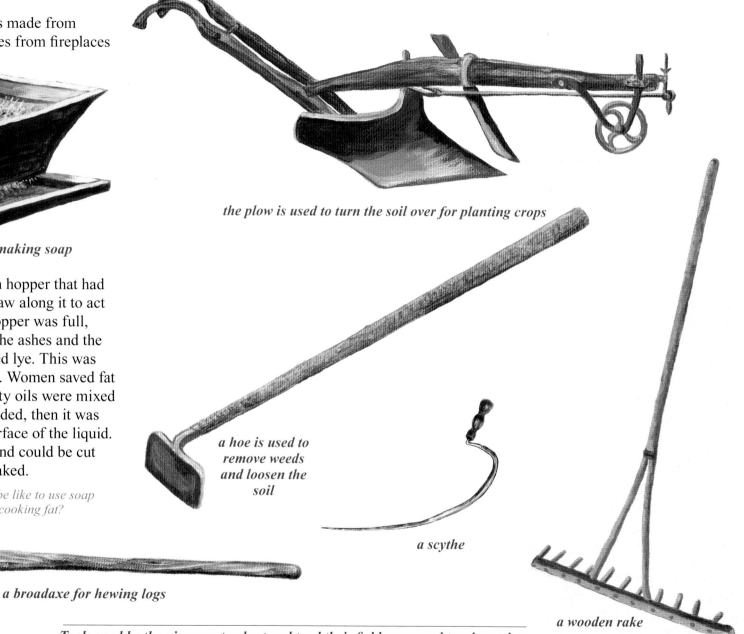

the plow is used to turn the soil over for planting crops

a hoe is used to remove weeds and loosen the soil

a scythe

a wooden rake

a broadaxe for hewing logs

Tools used by the pioneers to plant and tend their field crops and truck patches

31

Schools in Pittsburgh

Attempts were made as early as 1761 to start a school in Pittsburgh, but they didn't last long. Then in the November 10, 1786, issue of the *Pittsburgh Gazette*, a Mrs. Pride advertised a school for young ladies. Mrs. Pride said that she would teach needle-work, embroidering, reading, and English.[76] Young women learned the alphabet by sewing the letters with colored thread onto a stretched piece of cloth. This was called a sampler.

What would it be like to learn the alphabet by sewing letters on a piece of cloth?

Later, a boy's school was advertised. A Mr. Nickel said he would teach Latin, reading, English, writing, and arithmetic. In 1787 twenty-one men, including Mr. Brackenridge, started the "Pittsburgh Academy." Starting on April 13, 1789, Mr. George Welch began teaching at the new Academy. His lessons included "Learned Languages, English, Mathematics, Principles of Government."

The Academy included both boys and girls from 10 to 12 years old. They scheduled the classes to allow the children time to help with their family's farm work. Sometimes the children went to school at night, after working on their farms during the day. The custom of being off school during the summer months is a result of this need for children to help care for the family farm.

How would you feel going to school in the evening after working all day on your family's farm?

Vocabulary Words

goose quill pen

sampler

Classes were first held in a log cabin at the corner of Cherry Street and Third Avenue. The classroom was also the schoolmaster's bedroom, so desks were hung on a hinge on the wall so that they could be lowered at night. Benches were split logs. The students had to bring their own goose quill pens, homemade ink, and paper. Ink was used instead of pencils then. Pencils were very expensive at that time and contained broad pieces of lead that made very large marks on paper. If students came to evening classes, they also had to bring their own candles. Some schoolbooks were printed in Pittsburgh by Zadok Cramer. Others were brought from the east. Students who could not purchase school books often made their own by copy-ing the texts.

Recipes for Homemade Ink[77]

Brown Ink: Boil mashed walnuts or butternuts. Add vinegar and salt.

Black Ink: Add indigo or soot to brown mix.

Blue Ink: Mix powdered indigo (a plant) with madder (an herb), bran and water.

Soak then strain.

Lessons for Girls

Mrs. Pride taught young ladies to read and write English, needlework and embroidering.

What would it be like to copy your own schoolbooks?

In 1790, a two-story brick building was added to the school that had one room downstairs and two rooms upstairs. This school changed its appearance and location many more times and is known today as the University of Pittsburgh. As a reminder of its humble beginning, a log cabin sits on the lawn of the University of Pittsburgh's largest building, the Cathedral of Learning.[78]

Lessons for Boys

The classroom was also the teacher's bedroom, so desks were hung on hinges on the wall under a window for daylight, and so they could be lowered at night. Benches were split logs.

Some of the children's chores before and after school included preparing flax, which was grown for its fiber. Flax was used to make a linen cloth. After the flax was cut, it was dried in the sun and the seeds were beaten out. Then the flax was put into a Flax Break where it was broken into pieces. These were then beaten again (called "scutching.") with a flat board. This allowed the flax fibers to be pulled through a tool called a Hackle.

Flax Break

The Hackle had pointed metal spikes, which the flax was dragged through or combed through into strands. The larger strands were made into rough material for grain bags and heavy clothing. The smaller strands were spun on small spinning wheels to be woven into linen.[79] Linen was made into various clothing including shirts, shifts, hats, aprons, tablecloths, napkins, and sheets.

Flax Hackle

Hearth Toaster

On the hearth of some homes was a metal tool that held a rotating rack. Wire rods held pieces of bread in the rack that spun around when nudged. This act of spinning around was also called stirring. The tool was the original Toaster (Toast-Stir).[80]

Pattens

As Pittsburgh grew in size, wealth, and connections to the East, women in Pittsburgh began to wear the latest fashions of the time. To keep their expensive clothes from dipping into mud puddles, they wore *Pattens*. When they walked through the city, these acted as platforms to raise their shoes up above the muck.[81]

35

The Keelboats

In the 1780s, keelboats started to be made in Pittsburgh.[82] They were 50 to 80 feet long and narrow, pointed at both ends. Built on a heavy piece of lumber called a "keel," the frame of the keelboat was ribbed like a ship. Keelboats had runways on each side for pole-men to walk along and push the boat by using long metal tipped poles. They used from 6 to 18 boatmen on a keelboat, depending on its size. The boats were covered to protect cargo and passengers. A steer-man controlled the steering oar and gave orders to the pole men. Equal numbers of men worked on each side of the boat. The pole men pushed their pole down onto the river bottom when they heard the command "set." They would then walk along their runway pushing the boat forward against the river stream until they heard the command "lift."[83] The keelboats also had masts and sails, but sails could only be used when the wind blew from behind the boat. They had galley seats with oars to row with when needed.

How hard would you have to push to make a boat go upstream against the river current?

Sometimes the pole men used ropes to lasso tree branches along the shore and pulled the boat upstream by pulling on the ropes. These boats were used to transport cargo down the Ohio River and then back up to Pittsburgh. Travel down the Ohio River from Pittsburgh was much easier, helped by the river current flowing that way. To travel against the current to go up the Ohio River the pole-men had to push the boats and it took four times longer to travel in that direction.

Vocabulary Words

pole men

mast

sail

steer-man

upstream

downstream

36

How would you like to be a keelboat man?

By 1805, there were about 50 keelboats, each weighing 30 tons, transporting goods between Cincinnati and Pittsburgh.

Some boats traveling down from the Forks of the Ohio (Pittsburgh) were supplied to act as floating stores.[84] They stopped at river towns along the Ohio River and sold goods to the settlers living there. They would sound a tinhorn when they came near a town. Then all the people who had money to spend or goods to barter came rushing to the riverbank to purchase things that they couldn't make.

How would you feel if you heard the tin horn of a keelboat store coming to your river town?

The settlers often paid for their goods with what they had grown or made. This included corn, hams, dried pork, and animal hides.

37

Boat Building in Pittsburgh

Vocabulary Words

hardware

provision

pirate

steamboat

a mallet and mortise chisel for making mortise and tendon joints

By 1765, a boat yard was started in Pittsburgh. Packhorse trains from Philadelphia brought hardware for the boats. Lumber came from the dense woods of Pittsburgh. Although there was still great danger from Indian attacks, boats traveled down the Ohio to sell goods along the way. By 1783, boat builders on the Monongahela River near the village of Elizabeth advertised boats of all sizes and provisions of all kinds including flour. Between 1792 and 1800, many large sail boats and two row galley boats were built along the Monongahela River and sailed down the Ohio, then into the Mississippi River and passed New Orleans for use on the Atlantic Ocean.[85]

Boats traveling on the Ohio River before 1794 (before General Wayne's victory against the Indians) were in constant danger from both attacking Indians and river pirates.[86] On the Ohio River near Shawneetown, Illinois, was a group of river pirates sheltered by an overhanging cliff. They could see both up and down stream but were concealed themselves. They terrorized travelers on the route between Pittsburgh to New Orleans.

What do you think of the river Pirates?

In 1810, news of a steamboat traveling on the Hudson River reached Pittsburgh. The idea of inventing steamboats had been around since George Washington was shown a model of one built by James Rumsey in 1784. At the same time, a man named John Fitch had been also working on a steamboat of a different design. These two first inventors raced each other to perfect their boats for public use. Neither of them lived long enough to see this happen. Most people didn't believe that their idea of using steam power to move boats or land vehicles (cars and trains) could work. Other inventors carried on this quest for steam power and, eventually, after reviewing what others had already tried, Robert Fulton worked out the difficult problems to make steam engines powerful enough to use.[87]

Nicholas Roosevelt, a partner of Robert Fulton and Robert Livingston, who built that Hudson River steamboat, came to Pittsburgh in 1810 and built another steamboat on the Monongahela River, called the "New Orleans."[88] Roosevelt worked in a boat yard along the river at the bottom of Boyd's Hill. It took over a year to build, and when it was finished he had to wait until the spring thaw for water depth. Then in March of 1811, when the river water was deep enough, this side-wheeler steamboat was launched. On October 25, she began her maiden voyage that would take her to New Orleans. Traveling at 8 miles an hour, she steamed down the Monongahela and into the Ohio River heading towards the Mississippi.

After 1811, steamboat building became an important industry in Pittsburgh. In succeeding years, half of the boats traveling the Ohio and Mississippi Rivers were built in Pittsburgh.

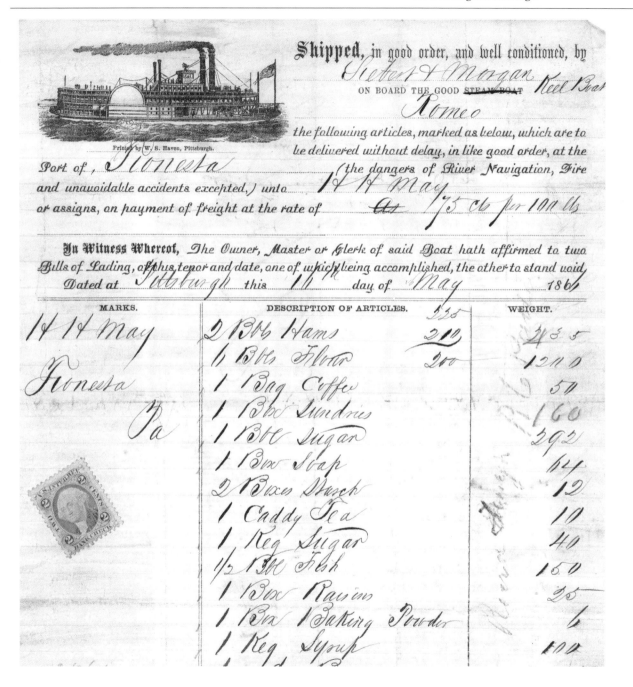

The first steamboats were hard to manage on curves in the river and were often stuck because they were too deep set for low water levels. This predicament was improved in 1816, when Captain Henry Shreve built the "Washington," a steamboat whose engine was stronger and whose boilers were up on the deck instead of below the water surface. He added an upper deck for passengers. He also invented a steamboat that removed dead trees (or sawyers) from the river, making navigation safer.

In 1839, the first large iron steamboat was built and called the "Valley Forge." In 1840, Pittsburgh built about one hundred iron boats. In 1857, a visitor counted 124 steamboats docked along the Monongahela wharf in Pittsburgh, with 30 steamboats arriving in a day.[89] The keelboat men were clearly upset by the steamboat. This new invention threatened their jobs. Soon the keelboats were used only for smaller streams that fed into the rivers.

If you were a keelboat man, why would you be upset about the steamboats?

There was a keel boater named Mike Fink who thought that Pittsburgh was getting too civilized and moved out to the Rocky Mountains to seek more adventure.

Mike Fink

Vocabulary Words

bragger

bully

Pittsburgh has become known for strong athletic teams. Perhaps the earliest of these could be called the "*Pittsburgh Keelers*." That is, the keelboat men. The most famous of these was Mike Fink.[90] He became an American legend alongside others like Davy Crockett, Daniel Boone, and John Henry. Mike Fink was a real person, born in 1770 near Fort Pitt.[91] He became a boatman as soon as he was old enough to be one. He first traveled by keelboat down the Ohio to St. Louis in 1814. When the river water was too low to navigate, he practiced sharp shooting. He became known as "bang all," and "the best shot in the country" because he easily could win any shooting match. Once, on a dare, he shot off the tails of eight pigs in a row from the keelboat as he passed them on the river. His best friend, John Carpenter, was also a great shot. They took turns shooting a cup of whiskey from off each other's heads. Mike was known as a bragger and bully, and he loved to tell jokes, insisting that everyone laugh at them.

Why was Mike Fink a bully?

He had a fondness for strong whiskey, which he shared with his admirers. He always had a fan club around him. He spoke in "boatman" dialogue. Davy Crockett described Mike Fink as "half horse and half alligator." Mike was heard to say, "I'm a salt river roarer, and I love the wimmin and I'm chock-full of fight."

What would make you afraid of Mike Fink?

Mike and his fellow boatmen were physically strong, wild characters who loved to get into wrestling fights where there were no rules. Many of them walked around with one eye missing, broken noses and bit-off ears. He was shot to death after admitting that he purposefully "missed" the whiskey cup and killed his friend Carpenter after they had an argument.[92]

Why would you let him shoot a cup off of your head?

After the Revolutionary War, not all the English soldiers sailed back to England. Even though King George III had agreed to withdraw all his soldiers from the United States in 1783, nine years later the British still had forts at Detroit, Michilimackinac, and Niagara.[93] English soldiers were trying to get the Indians to fight the Americans in what was called the Northwest Territory.[94] which was the land north of the Ohio River. The English gave the Indians guns and told them that they would help them fight the Americans and make them leave. At that time, everything west of Pittsburgh was considered the *"wild west."* The American General Anthony Wayne fought the Indians for the land north of the Ohio River, called the Northwest Territory. This territory eventually became five states including Ohio, Indiana, Illinois, Michigan and Wisconsin.

What made the settlers keep moving west to live?

When the final battle happened in 1794, outside of an English Fort called Fallen Timbers (where the city of Toledo, Ohio is located), the English soldiers didn't help the Indians. Instead of fighting with them, the English locked themselves inside their Fort. They could not risk starting another war with the Americans.[95]

Why did the British help the Indians fight the Americans after the Revolutionary War?

Some of the Pioneers coming west in America had been given land deeds as payment for being soldiers during the Revolutionary War. After that war, the new United States of America could only pay their debts in Continental paper money, which had no value in gold or silver.[96] For that reason it was mostly considered worthless paper. Pennsylvania gave "Depreciation Lands" to these Veterans as payment instead of money, because paper money had "depreciated," or lost value during the Revolutionary War. These Depreciation Lands were in the "V" formed between the Allegheny and Ohio Rivers, beginning at the Forks of the Ohio north of Pittsburgh.

How would you feel if you were paid in land instead of money for doing your job?

The one big opportunity that a veteran soldier had was the land given to him. Although a lot of the veterans did come west and become farmers, many sold some or all of their land to earn real money that they needed to care for themselves and their families.[97]

Errata

Regretfully, the author must point out that a typo has occurred on page 41 of the book.
Left column, last paragraph reads:

When the final battle happened in 1794, outside of an English Fort called Fallen Timbers (where the city of Toledo, Ohio is located),

Should read:

When the final battle happened in 1794, outside of an English Fort called Miami at Fallen Timbers (where the city of Toledo, Ohio is located),

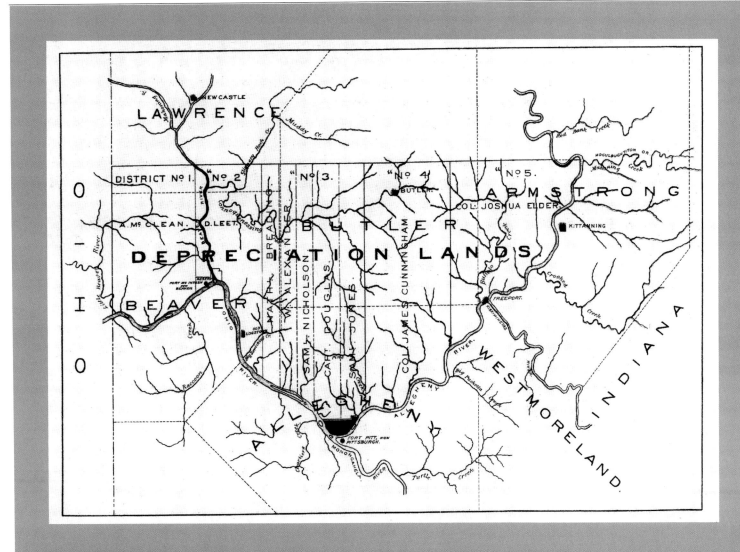

Many contemporary parcels of property in Allegheny, Armstrong, Beaver, and Butler Counties can relate their boundaries to the original Depreciation Lands. For example, Reilly's Summer Seat Farm, northwest of Pittsburgh, is situated on a track of land granted to a Richard Somers back in July of 1786.

Johnny Appleseed

In 1794, Jonathan Chapman, known better as "Johnny Appleseed," came to Pittsburgh from Connecticut. At first he worked along the river helping build flatboats to carry pioneers further west along the Ohio River. He stayed for 12 years in a log cabin on Grant's Hill, and his home became a shelter for the homeless. He decided to share his ability to grow apples. He made a special boat, constructed of two birch-bark canoes lashed together, and he loaded them with bags of apple seeds.

What would make you want to meet Johnny Appleseed?

He traveled down the Ohio River and through Indian country making friends and teaching people (both settlers and Indians) how to grow apples.

What did the Native Americans think of Johnny Appleseed?

He also planted medicinal herbs that were used as medicine for sickness and taught what he knew about these early "cures." Today some of our medicines come from these same herbs.[98]

Vocabulary Words

cure

herb

a clamp for joining pieces of wood

a plow plane for making groves in wood

The Whiskey Rebellion

Recipe for Johnny Cake:

Two cups cornmeal, one-cup wheat,

One-cup good eggs that you can eat,

One-half cup molasses too,

One big spoon sugar added thereto,

Salt and soda, each a small spoon,

Mix up quickly and bake it soon.[99]

From Brenner,

My Folks Come in a Covered Wagon

Vocabulary Words

excise tax

excise men

revenue

license

Johnny Cake

corn pone

tarred and feathered

Among the crops that grew easily and in abundance for early Pittsburgh Pioneers was corn and rye. Corn was used for many things. The Pioneer diet daily included various forms of corn including Johnnycakes, corn-meal mush, corn pone, corn bread, corn sticks, roasted corn, and popcorn. Corn also fed the animals. The corncob was made into pipes. Corn shucks made baby dolls.

Cooks made baking powder from the ashes of corncobs.[100]

Rye was not as versatile. It could of course be made into bread. The other major use for it was it could be made into whiskey. The Pittsburgh Pioneers wanted to ship the extra rye they grew back east to exchange for other goods. The only reliable transportation available then was packhorse train. They soon discovered that one packhorse could carry 24 bushels of rye made into whiskey compared to only four bushels of rye as grain.[101] There was very little money in circulation in Pioneer Pittsburgh. A gallon of whiskey was considered worth a shilling. It was used the same as cash to purchase goods, and even purchase land.[102] In early Pittsburgh there was no license needed to sell whiskey or beer. Then, in 1791, after the Revolutionary War, the United States Government attempted to enforce a whiskey tax.[103] Taxes were set for anyone selling distilled whiskey. The local Pittsburgh farmers disagreed with the tax and refused to pay. Tax collectors, called "Excise men" or "revenue collectors," came to farms demanding tax payment. The farmers were furious that the government did this. They felt that the government had done little to help them when they needed protection from the Indians, and the government had not been able to pay the soldiers who had fought in the Revolutionary War. The farmers were also poor and had no cash money to pay the taxes. If they did pay the taxes, the farmer would make no profit from his work. The Western Pennsylvania farmers considered the Whiskey Tax wrong the same way that revolutionary

Angry farmers marched to General John Neville's plantation to demand that he resign his job as Tax Collector.

patriots considered the Tea Tax wrong. People who did not live where they lived were taxing them; they had no representatives in the government to officially protest or prevent these taxes.[104]

Why did the United States Government charge a Whiskey Tax on the Pioneer farmers in Pittsburgh?

The farmers were so upset they tarred and feathered some of the Excise men. General John Neville was the local Pittsburgh inspector for this Excise Tax. He lived on a ten-thousand acre plantation that he called Bower Hill. While most of his neighbors were small farmers who still lived in log cabins, General Neville's house was two stories high. It had plaster walls with wall paper, carpet on polished hardwood floors, fine furniture, mirrors, fine china, silverware, crystal glassware, a Franklin stove, and framed pictures.[105]

The rebellious farmers marched on his house demanding that he resign from this job. Soldiers were guarding the General's home. A fight started, and a bullet killed one of the protesters. The crowd set fire to the General's house and barn. It was reported that at the request of Neville's slaves, they did not burn his row of slave houses.[106] Other accounts say that General Neville's mansion and all but one of his out buildings were burned.[107]

If you were a farmer would you burn down General Neville's house?

Two weeks later, 5,000 farmers gathered in Braddock's field and marched towards Pittsburgh. They knew that those who agreed with

the Excise Tax lived and worked there. They were ready to burn down Pittsburgh. Fortunately, several men were able to persuade them to calm down. They setup tables of food and drink and invited them to sit and talk. Hugh H. Brackenridge said that the visit of the "Whisky Boys," as he called them, to Pittsburgh "cost him four barrels of old whisky."[108]

In October of 1794, President Washington sent 13,000 soldiers to put down the rebellion. But by the time they arrived, the farmers had given up their fight. Two of their leaders were caught and brought to trial in the east. Although they were found guilty, President Washington pardoned them.[109]

Later on President Thomas Jefferson repealed the Whiskey Tax that President Washington had sent an army to insist upon.[110]

Can you think of any other taxes that are not popular today?

Meriwether Lewis and William Clark

On July 15, 1803, a man named Meriwether Lewis came to Pittsburgh. Knowing that Pittsburgh was the boat building center for travelers heading west, he had ordered a keelboat to be built there. Mr. Lewis needed a strong, large keelboat to carry supplies for his expedition. He had been hired by President Thomas Jefferson to explore, survey, and make maps of the new part of the United States. President Jefferson had just bought what was called the Louisiana Territory, also called the Northwest Territory, from France. This addition of land doubled the size of the country. Today, the Northwest Territory includes the States of Ohio, Indiana, Illinois, Michigan, Wisconsin and part of Minnesota.

No one knew exactly what the new land looked like. They hoped to find a river passage through the Northwest Territory that connected to the Ohio or Mississippi Rivers that would take them all the way to the Pacific Ocean. They called this route the Northwest Passage.

Meriwether Lewis had been to Pittsburgh before. He was part of the Virginia army that President George Washington sent to stop the Whiskey Rebellion in 1794.[111]

Arriving in Pittsburgh in 1803, Lewis found that his boat was behind schedule. The boat builder was very slow and unreliable. Fortunately, a well-built keelboat was finally finished. In October, Lewis sailed down the Ohio from Pittsburgh with men he had hired. Because the water was so low, they had great difficulty getting the new keelboat down the Ohio River. Lewis would need to wait for the spring thaw to continue. He intended to take the boat to St. Louis where he would join his co-captain for the expedition, William Clark. There they intended to finish buying and loading provisions for their trip. By then it was so late in the year, they had to wait until spring to continue their journey. On May 14, 1804, Lewis and Clark along with their crew began their journey. It would take them three years and many dangerous adventures to travel all the way to the Pacific Ocean and back.

What would make you want to go with Lewis and Clark to explore the new part of the United States?

Lewis and Clark were fortunate to have a 14 year old Native American women named Sacagawea lead them across to her tribe at the foot of the Rocky Mountains. They discovered that there wasn't a river connection to make a Northwest Passage. They had to carry their supplies between rivers and over the Rocky Mountains. They were very lucky to find friendly Indian Tribes that helped them survive.[112]

What would it be like to not be able to communicate with anyone from home for three years?

Vocabulary Word

communicate

The Allegheny Portage Railroad

Vocabulary Words

merchant

canal

inclined plane

ascend

descend

funicular

aqueduct

The merchants in the big cities along the east coast of the United States soon realized how good it was for their businesses to sell their goods to people along the Ohio River. The need to make travel faster and easier caused some to consider other ways to get to the west instead of the poor roads that did exist. Some thought about making a water route to speed the trip. Since rivers did not connect all the way from east to west, they decided to make canals between the rivers so boats could travel across. It was the states that had to supply the money to make canal building happen. The first state to do this was New York. They built the Erie Canal to connect Lake Erie to the Hudson River, which flows to New York City. Pennsylvania realized that they needed to act quickly so their claim as the way to the west through Pittsburgh would continue.

This brought about the Main Line of Public Works, which was a combination railroad and canal system that linked Philadelphia to Pittsburgh.[113] Construction of the Main Line began in 1826 and was completed in 1834. Travel began in Philadelphia on a railroad to Columbia, PA (near Lancaster, PA). There, freight and people were put onto canal boats that traveled up to the Juniata River. The boats crossed into the Juniata canal floating west until they reached Hollidaysburg. This is where the Allegheny Mountains began. To make the trip up and over the mountains, the Allegheny Portage Railroad was built. Travel time from Philadelphia to Pittsburgh changed from 23 days by stagecoach to just 4 days using the Main Line system.

How would it feel to take only 4 days to travel between Philadelphia and Pittsburgh instead of over 20 days?

The Allegheny Portage Railroad was a 36-mile funicular railroad.[114] A funicular is a cable railway, up or down a mountain in which an ascending car counterbalances a descending car. It was a series of 10 inclined planes, five to go up one side of the Mountains and five to come down the other side. The canal boats were built in sections and disconnected so each section could be pulled onto a railroad type flat car. These cars were part of double track cable railways. On one track, three cars would ascend, and on the other track, three other cars would descend that part of the system. Steam engines powered the cables that pulled these cars up or down. The cables were first made of hemp rope, but there were many accidents because the ropes often broke from pulling the heavy canal boats up or down the mountains. John Roebling (who lived near Pittsburgh in Saxonburg) invented twisted steel wire ropes to use on the Portage Railroad instead of the hemp ropes.[115] This made the trip much safer. First horses, and later steam locomotive engines would pull the cable cars along the flat land then to the next inclined plane. At one part, the cable cars were pulled through the Staple Bend Tunnel, the first railroad tunnel built in the United States, and through part of the Allegheny Mountains. When all the parts of the canal boat finally reached Johnstown, they were reconnected and traveled again on a canal to the Allegheny River. They crossed the Allegheny River at Freeport and traveled beside the River to Pittsburgh's North Side. There, a long 1,140-foot aqueduct ran over the Allegheny River to downtown Pittsburgh.[116] The main depot was on the corner of Grant and Seventh, and a turning basin ran between Penn and Liberty Avenue. An extension of the canal ran under Grants Hill through a tunnel to the Monongahela River. This tunnel was built in hopes that it would eventually connect to another canal system being built towards Pittsburgh through Maryland.

The cost to travel by the canal system was half the cost of a stagecoach trip. The cost of sending goods along the canal system was much less expensive than bringing them by a Conestoga wagon. The canal was a great help to the economy of Pittsburgh.[117] When the Pennsylvania Railroad began operating

passenger trains between Philadelphia and Pittsburgh, in 1854, the trip took just fifteen hours.[118]

What would be fun about floating across Pennsylvania in a canal boat?

The canal system was still used to haul freight for a while, but people preferred to use the faster railroad to travel. Two inclined planes are still in use in Pittsburgh today, The Duquesne Incline and the Mon (Monongahela) Incline, use steel wires. Steel wires were used in suspension bridges that Roebling designed and built across the Monongahela River at Smithfield Street, and across the Al-

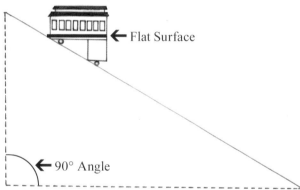

← Flat Surface

← 90° Angle

legheny River at Sixth Street in Pittsburgh.[119] John Roebling and his son, Washington Roebling, used steel wires to build the Brooklyn Bridge that connects Manhattan Island to Brooklyn in New York City.

Although the canal system was a great improvement in transportation, it didn't take long for it to be replaced in transporting peo-

ple between Philadelphia and Pittsburgh. The Pennsylvania Railroad (PRR) began service between those cities in Pennsylvania as early as 1852. By 1859, the PRR bought the canals in Pennsylvania. The canal system continued to be used to haul freight, but passengers preferred traveling on the railroad.[120]

Which would be the better way to travel? By canal, or by railroad, and why?

Because the Allegheny Portage Railroad happened, Pittsburgh continued to be the main Port through which passengers and cargo moved between East and West in the United States.

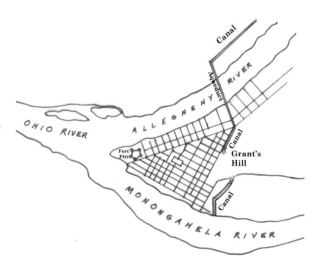

George Anshutz

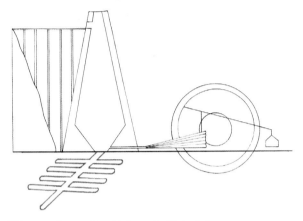

The trades of Pittsburgh listed in Cramer's 1804 Almanac included "Ironmongery." This meant that iron and steel tools, like axes, hoes, augers, chisels, and drawing knives were made in Pittsburgh.[121]

In 1793, George Anshutz started the first Iron Furnace on Two Mile Run, in Shadyside, close to where the Winchester Thurston School is now situated. He made cast iron stoves and grates.

Iron ore was found in abundance in Pennsylvania. Iron ore lay on top and near the surface of ground at the Forks of the Ohio.[122] *However, the few roads that did exist made it too expensive to haul iron ore to this location. The Anshutz business closed after just one year of operation.*[123]

Large amounts of materials were needed to make iron because an iron furnace operated 24 hours a day, seven days a week for at least 9 months at a time. The ingredients to make iron were charcoal, limestone, and iron ore. Even though there were many large trees on this land near the Forks, the wood from the trees needed first to be turned into charcoal before it could be used to make iron. An acre of trees was needed to produce enough charcoal to fire an iron furnace for 24 hours.[124] Piles of wood being charred into charcoal were a common sight. The wood was stacked into a cone. The center had sticks that were 3 to 4 inches wide and 6 feet high. Other bundles of sticks were laid around this until the bottom of the circle was about 25 feet in diameter. Damp leaves and dirt were put on the sides and holes were poked into the sides to draw air in. Then the top of the pile was set on fire. The pile needed to be watched carefully for the 3 to 10 days that it took to become charcoal. If any flames were seen in the pile, they needed to be smothered so that the wood burned slowly into charcoal instead of burning quickly into ashes.[125] The piles of charcoal gave off heavy black smoke that smelled bad, and many towns made it a law that these piles could only be lit outside of the main part of towns where people lived.[126]

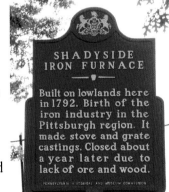

SHADYSIDE IRON FURNACE
Built on lowlands here in 1792. Birth of the iron industry in the Pittsburgh region. It made stove and grate castings. Closed about a year later due to lack of ore and wood.
PENNSYLVANIA HISTORICAL AND MUSEUM COMMISSION

The iron furnaces were usually built into the side of a small hill near a stream of water. The water turned a wooden wheel that operated a huge bellows to blow air into the furnace and make the fire burn hot enough to melt the iron ore. Bricks lined the furnace stack, which was shaped like a cone with the large part on the ground sitting on a hearth. A small wooden bridge was built across from the top of the hill to an opening near the top of the furnace stack where workmen could constantly keep feeding the fire of the furnace. Men filled these furnaces with alternate layers of charcoal, iron ore, and limestone measured in basket or bucket loads. The ore melted into a liquid and dropped down to the hearth below. Cinders or slag floated on top of the liquid (molten) iron, and was drawn off. About twice a day, the molten iron was run out into casting beds of wet sand in wood frames. There was a main casting bed called the sow, with smaller little beds coming out of shoots around it called pigs. An early iron master thought these looked like a mother pig with her litter of suckling pigs. For this reason the iron became known as pig iron. Before the iron cooled, the pigs were separated from the sow. They then could be sent to blacksmiths to be made into many useful tools.[127]

Martin Delany

In Pittsburgh, one of the best and most popular taverns was on the corner of Second and Ferry Streets and was operated by a black man named Charles Richards. He was the son of Benjamin Richards who had come to Pittsburgh with General Forbes and George Washington. Benjamin Richards was wealthy and prosperous by his cattle dealership and butcher business having contracts to supply the local military forts with his meats. He owned a house on the corner of Third and Chancery Lane. Both Benjamin and Charles were leading businessmen of Pittsburgh and, along with two other free black men, also successful businessmen, signed the 1787 Petition that helped create Allegheny County.[128] Charles Richards married Felicia Fitzgerald and their daughter Katherine Richards married Martin Delany.[129]

Vocabulary Word

abolition

Dr. Martin Delany came to Pittsburgh in 1831. He studied medicine with Dr. Andrew McDowell, Dr. Francis LeMoyne, and Dr. Joseph Gazzam. He then studied at Harvard Medical School until a petition by white students there had all African Americans removed.

Why did the white students make the black students, including Martin Delany, leave Harvard Medical School?

Back in Pittsburgh, Delany trained himself to be a writer and public speaker. He started and edited an abolition paper called The Mystery, and helped Frederick Douglas write and edit publications. In 1865 Delany met with President Abraham Lincoln and convinced him to form a regiment of black men, under black officers as part of the Union Army. He became a Major in this regiment, making him the highest-ranking African American Officer in the United States Military. His son also served in that regiment.[130]

There were some people who were held as slaves in Pittsburgh. Slavery was very small here compared to the Southern States. The 1790 United States Census showed there were 40 slaves among the 1,853 people then living in Pittsburgh.[131]

Frontier Pittsburgh and all of Western Pennsylvania practiced social equality. For a while there was no difference in social importance between free white and free black people in Pittsburgh that existed elsewhere.[132] Some wealthy white men, especially those who owned larger farms, brought slaves to help work them. Although most slaves in Pittsburgh at first worked on farms, later on some worked in town as shoemakers, blacksmiths, barbers, cooks, wool spinners, clothes dyers and seamstresses, tavern workers, millers, etc.

If you had a choice, what business would you want to own or work at in downtown Pittsburgh?

There was not opposition in Pittsburgh to educate slaves as there was in the South.[133] In 1780, an Abolition of Slavery law in Pennsylvania meant people born to slaves would be free, but the law allowed for a 28 year time period during which the newborns would be considered indentured instead of being slaves.[134]

The Mystery

The Great Fire of Pittsburgh

Vocabulary Words

Volunteer Fire Company

reservoir

water pressure

fire hose

merchandise

record

cornice

disaster

cinder

On April 10, 1845, a fire spread throughout downtown Pittsburgh, destroying one third of the city. It hadn't rained for weeks before this, and a dusty strong wind had been blowing. Around noon that day, near the corner of Second Avenue and Ferry Street, a woman had made a fire outside and began to boil water to wash clothes. The wind blew straw into the fire, causing it to grow quickly and spread to an ice house next door. Then the adjoining wooden buildings caught fire. It spread across the street to a cotton factory. It moved quickly because the dry wind blew cinders onto the wooden buildings.

There were nine volunteer fire companies in Pittsburgh with shiny metal engines, much larger than the little wooden fire pumper used in the early years at Fort Pitt. These were still just hand pumpers, and there were only two water main pipes, a 6-inch main on Third Street and an 8-inch main on Liberty. The reservoir on Quarry (Herron) Hill was low because of the dry weather. The firefighters couldn't stop the fire because of low water pressure, and also because many of the leather fire hoses were ripped and leaking.[135] At first firefighters had some success, but as they pumped water with their hand pumped engines, the water pressure slowed down from a stream into a muddy dribble. Many citizens helped the firefighters. They began bucket brigades to refill the hand pumpers, but by this time the fire was out of control. The firefighters used pry bars to rip off burning cornices from churches. Because Pittsburgh was a large port for merchandise moving west, there were many warehouses that stored goods. People began moving their goods onto the wharf along the Monongahela, but the fire soon spread to the River's edge, burning these piles of merchandise.

What would you do if you saw a fire burning houses on its way towards you?

Steamboats anchored along the Monongahela River cast off to save themselves and their cargo. The largest hotel in Pittsburgh was the Monongahela House on the corner of Smithfield and Water Streets. When the walls of this hotel fell down in flames, cinders flew onto the wooden Smithfield Street Bridge. Within 10 minutes, the bridge that crossed from downtown Pittsburgh to Birmingham (the South Side) was in flames and fell into the River.[136]

The Neptunes had just arrived at the scene. John yelled, "Look at this!" in disbelief as he shook the nozzle in his hands. Water that had begun to spray out of the hose as his pump men worked the levers back and forth had suddenly turned into a slow drip. There would be no more water coming from the dried out reservoir on Quarry Hill that day. Later the firefighters would learn that part of the main line had collapsed obstructing what little water was left to pump.

One third of downtown Pittsburgh was destroyed in the fire, from Ferry (Stanwix) Street to Ross Street, and from Water (Fort Pitt Boulevard) Street to Fourth Avenue. Fortunately, this happened in daylight and only two lives were lost.[137] Although the Pittsburgh Academy had become the University of Pittsburgh by then, and now was in a stone building, it was one of the buildings destroyed in that fire.[138] All the paper records inside the school were burned in the fire. Many businesses never recovered after the fire. They didn't have enough money to replace what had been burned.

What would it be like to lose all of your things in a fire?

Even some of the fire insurance companies were destroyed. They couldn't pay money to people who had policies with them.[139] Donations of money from around the country were sent to help Pittsburgh residents. Many of the survivors helped each other as they could.

Would you open your home to people after a major disaster?

The Court House, warehouses, and private homes were opened to people who became homeless from the fire. It was not long before Pittsburgh rebuilt and continued to be the great Port to the West.

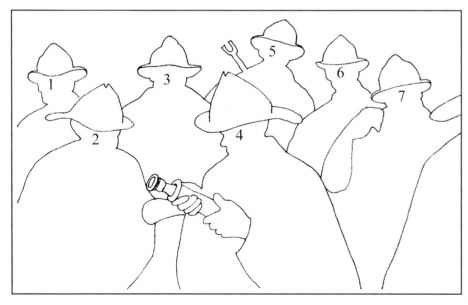

Firefighters modeled in the painting of the 1845 Pittsburgh Fire are actual City of Pittsburgh Firefighters who are related to the author.

1. Chief Jack McKeown
2. Chief Ed Seger
3. Captain Mike Steinbaugh
4. Captain John Steinbaugh
5. Captain Mike Rinozzi*
6. Captain Harry McKeown
7. Hoseman Tony Caiaccia

_____

* City of Chicago Firefighter

Interesting People of Early Pittsburgh

By 1790 the population of Pittsburgh included:

37% English,

7% Welsh,

17% Scotch,

19% Irish,

12% German,

and the remaining 8% were other Nationalities.

Many streets, small Boroughs and buildings in Pittsburgh were named for some of these early Pittsburgh people.

Queen Aliquippa [23] – Aliquippa, Pennsylvania was named after her. She was the Queen of the Seneca Indians, who George Washington first visited in 1753.

Tarleton Bates [140] – Bates Street was named after Tarleton Bates, who came to Pittsburgh when he was 18 years old from Virginia. He was a government worker and was co-owner and editor of the Tree of Liberty newspaper. He was challenged to a duel after a political argument with the publisher of a weekly newspaper. This duel occurred in Oakland in a ravine called three-mile run (the upper end becomes Bates Street). Bates was shot in the chest and died an hour later. He is buried in Trinity Churchyard.

Colonel Henry Bouquet [55] – Bouquet Street was named for Colonel Henry Bouquet who won the Battle of Bushy Run, after which the Indians moved away and didn't attack Fort Pitt again.

John Boyd [141] – Boyd's Hill, now where Duquesne University and Mercy Hospital are located, was named after John Boyd who was co-owner of the Pittsburgh Gazette with John Scull after Joseph Hall died. In 1788, Boyd tried unsuccessfully to establish a public library in Pittsburgh.

Hugh Henry Brackenridge [67, 78 108 142] – Brackenridge, PA, was named after Hugh Henry Brackenridge. A lawyer, writer, politician, large land owner, founder of the second newspaper in Pittsburgh called *"The Tree of Liberty,"* and one of the founders of the Pittsburgh Academy that became the University of Pittsburgh.

General Edward Braddock [29] – Braddock, PA, and Braddock Avenue were named after General Edward Braddock, who was killed trying to capture Fort Duquesne from the French in 1755.

Dr. Felix Brunot [143] – Dr. Felix Brunot, who came to Pittsburgh in 1797, named Brunot's Island. He had come with Lafayette from France and was a surgeon in the Revolutionary War. He lived on and owned Brunot's Island, but his office was on Liberty in Pittsburgh.

Zadok Cramer [62, 64] – became the first book publisher in Pittsburgh. He annually printed Almanacks and updated copies of *"The Navigator,"* a guide of how to travel down the Ohio River by boat.

Major Isaac Craig [70, 144, 145] – Craig Street was named for Major Isaac Craig who co-founded the first glasswork factory in Pittsburgh.

George Croghan [16, 27, 28] – Known as the "King of the Traders" had his main fur-trading store in Fort Pitt.

Martin Delany [129, 130] – A doctor, writer and public speaker, he wrote and edited abolition publications. He served as the highest-ranking African American Officer in the United States Army during the Civil War.

Christopher Gist [21] – Gist Street was named after Christopher Gist, the frontier guide who led George Washington to meet with various Indian Chiefs. General Braddock died at Gist's farm near Uniontown.

Major James Grant [31] – Grant Street was named after Major James Grant who came to Pittsburgh with General Forbes. He and his Scottish soldiers, who wore kilts, unsuccessfully tried to take Fort Duquesne away from the French.

Guyasuta [48] – The Guyasuta Boy Scout Camp in Sharpsburg is named after this Native American Chief who both helped George Washington as a guide and then tried to stop the English from coming to live in his homeland at the Forks of the Ohio.

Jacob Haymaker [146] – Haymaker Street is named for Jacob Haymaker, a boat-builder, whose boat yard was on Pittsburgh's south side.

John Marie [147] – owned Marie's Tavern on Grant's Hill. It was a large, well-cared-for Tavern on six acres overlooking the town of Pittsburgh and often used for important meetings. Marie was 75 years old when he sold Grant's Hill to James Ross, a Senator from Pennsylvania.

Alexander McKee [148] – McKee's Rocks was named for Alexander McKee, an early Fur Trader in Pittsburgh. He was a Tory during the American Revolution and escaped to Detroit where he worked for the British.

Alexander Negley and Jacob Negley [149] – Negley Avenue was named for Alexander and his son, Jacob Negley, both rich farmers.

General John Neville [105, 106, 107] – Neville Street and Neville Island were named for General John Neville. He was the Excise man who had the misfortune of having his house burned down after trying to enforce the Whiskey Tax on Pittsburgh farmers in 1794.

General James O'Hara [70, 144, 145, 147] – O'Hara Township was named after General James O'Hara, a Fur Trader, then Revolutionary War General. He co-founded the first glasswork factory in Pittsburgh. Throughout his life he also owned two tanneries, a sawmill, an iron furnace, a shipbuilding yard, and the first brewery in Pittsburgh, called the Point Brewery (near the Block House) where he used glass bottles from his factory to bottle beer.

Benjamin Richards [128] – a free Black man, he came to Pittsburgh with General Forbes. He made a fortune as a butcher, provisioning military posts. He owned a large amount of property in early Pittsburgh.

Charles Richards [128, 129] – Son of Benjamin Richards, he owned a Tavern at the corner of Second and Ferry Streets. He and his father along with two other free Blacks signed a Petition in 1787 that led to the creation of Allegheny County.

Senator James Ross [150] – Ross Street was named for Senator James Ross.

Jonas Roup [151] – Roup Street was named for Jonas Roup, a rich farmer.

Mary Schenley [56] – Schenley Park was a gift from Mary Croghan Schenley, the Granddaughter of James O'Hara.

General John Stanwix [65] – Stanwix Street was named after General John Stanwix who finished building Fort Pitt.

Jane Grey Swisshelm [139] – Swisshelm is named after her. She published and edited four newspapers between 1847 and 1866, and was an abolitionist and women's rights sponsor.

Conrad Winebiddle [146, 149] – Winebiddle Street was named after Conrad Winebiddle, a rich farmer and property owner.

Colonel George Woods [59] – Wood Street was named after the man, Colonel George Woods, who made the first street plan of Pittsburgh's downtown.

Vocabulary Words

Abolition – The abolishing of slavery.

Almanack (also spelled almanac and almanach – A publication (usually a printed book) for a one year's time including different general information about that year.

Ally, Allies – To enter into a union or association with others for a mutual goal as a helper.

Ancestors – A group of grandparents from whom a person is descended.

Aqueduct – A canal built up over a river or hollow of land.

Army Regular – A soldier in a regular, established army where being a soldier is his full-time job.

Ascend – Rise up to a higher level.

Axe – A cutting tool with a heavy edged head attached to a handle, used for chopping and splitting wood, felling trees.

Bastion – A projecting area of a fortification, part of a fort that is the strongest area.

Blacksmith – A smith who forges iron (black metal).

Bookbinder – Someone who binds pieces of paper together to form a book.

Bragger – A loud, arrogant boaster who calls attention to themselves. They have exaggerated pride in their own accomplishments and glorify themselves.

Buckskin – The skin of a buck or deer (suede finished leather).

Bully – Someone who forces others to do what they want by treating them badly.

Canal – A man-made waterway over which boats were drawn by animals, usually mules. Beside the canal was a towpath on which the mules pulled the boat along by a long rope attached to the front of the boat.

Caulk/Caulking – A tapered piece put in between a structure, as caulk used to seal in between wooden boards.

Cargo – Goods of merchandise (things to sell) also called freight that is transported by land, water, and air.

Chaff – The seed covering and other debris separated from the seed in threshing grain.

Cinder – A piece of partly burned material from a fire, capable of still burning.

Colonial Governor – An official placed to govern or control a Colony.

Colonist – A member of a colony that settles in a new country.

Colonize – To establish in residence.

Colony – A group of people living in a new territory that keeps ties to the parent state.

Communicate – To pass information from one person to another.

Cornmeal – Meal ground from corn to use for cooking.

Corn pone – Corn bread made without milk or eggs and baked or fried.

Corn shuck – To peel off the outer leaves of an ear of corn.

Conestoga Wagon – A broad wheeled, covered wagon usually drawn by six horses to transport freight or cargo (originally made in Conestoga, PA near Lancaster, PA).

Continental Money – Paper money printed by one of the American Colonies to use as money or currency for exchange or trading of goods.

Cooper – Someone who makes or repairs wooden casks, barrels, or tubs.

Cornice – A band of wood or metal for decoration along the top edge of an inside or outside building wall.

Cure – To restore health, to bring about recovery from illness.

Debris – Pieces of broken apart things, rubbish.

Depreciate – To lower the price or estimated value of.

Depreciation Land – Land given to Revolutionary War Veterans instead of money to pay them for being soldiers.

Descend – To pass from a higher place to a lower one.

Disaster – A sudden great misfortune or loss.

Dry goods – Cloth and ready to wear clothes.

Excise men – An officer appointed to rate and collect taxes.

Fee – A fixed charge or price.

Ferry – A boat that transports people, animals or materials across a body of water.

Fire Hose – A flexible tube to transport water onto a fire to put it out.

Flatboat – A boat with a flat bottom used for transportation in shallow waters.

Forge – A furnace where metal is heated in a workshop, where iron is made malleable (bendable).

Fort – A place erected to defend or strengthen, made strong to defend attacks, usually occupied by army troops.

Fort Necessity – A quickly built stockade of logs, built by George Washington at a place called Great Meadows, to protect and defend his army from French soldiers.

Foundry Type – Metal Type used in a hand printing press that has been cast into letters in a foundry by heating the metal until it is liquid and pouring it into molds.

French and Indian War – A war fought both in the United States and in Europe (called the Seven Years War in Europe) between England and France over ownership of territory.

Funicular – A cable railway up or down a mountain in which an ascending car counterbalances a descending car.

Fur pelt – Skin of an animal with fur or wool still attached.

Fur Trader – A person whose business is to trade goods in return for fur pelts.

Hand Printing Press – A hand-operated printing press that presses paper against metal letters that have been inked. This causes the ink to become letters on the paper.

Hames – Curved supports attached to the harness of draft horses (horses that draw or pull loads).

Hardware – Fittings, tools, utensils or parts of machines made of metal for particular purposes.

Herb - A plant used for its medicinal qualities.

Hoe – A tool with a thin, flat blade on a long handle for loosening earth, especially around plants.

Immemorial – Before anyone can remember.

Immigrant – A person who comes to a new country to live permanently.

Inclined Plane – A flat surface moving along an angle that is between 90 to 180 degrees.

Indenture – A formal document binding one person to work for another for a given period of time.

Keelboat – A shallow covered riverboat built along a curved wooden keel (wooden curved beam along the bottom) usually used to transport cargo.

Land Speculator – A person who takes the risk of buying land in the hope of selling it to make a profit.

License – Permission by authority to act or engage in a business.

Maddox – A hand tool with a flat blade and long handle used to dig ditches in the dirt.

Maintenance – The upkeep of property or equipment.

Malster/Brewer – Someone who makes grain into malt and brews beer or ale.

Mason Dixon Line – A geographic line made by surveyors Charles Mason and Jeremiah Dixon between 1763 and 1767 to resolve an argument about Colonial borders. This line formed the borders between what is now the States of Pennsylvania, Maryland, Delaware and West Virginia. The Mason Dixon Line symbolized the boundary between the Northern States and the Southern States.

Mast – A long pole rising from the deck of a ship to support a sail.

Merchant – A buyer or seller of goods for profit, a storekeeper.

Migrate – To move from one country, or place, to another.

Navigate – To steer a course through, to make your way through to a destination.

Orderly grid – A uniform space of horizontal (left to right) and perpendicular (up to down) lines that form an organized mesh.

Pack Horse – A horse used to transport cargo on its back.

Pacifism/Pacifist – Someone who opposes war or violence as a way to settle disputes and because of this belief, he refuses to go to war as a soldier.

Parallel – Moving so that corresponding movements go together at the same time and stay apart at the same distance.

Patriot – A person who loves his/her country and works to support it.

Pentagon – A structure with five equal angles and five sides.

Petition – A formal, written request to do something.

Pioneer – One of the first people to settle in a territory.

Pirate – Someone who is a robber on the water.

Plow – A tool used to cut, lift, and turn over soil to prepare it to plant seeds in it.

Pole men – Men who used poles on flatboats and keelboats to push to boat through the water.

Port – A harbor town or city where ships may take on or put off cargo. Also the port of entry (the opening into something).

Postmaster – One who has charge of a Post Office.

Proprietor – Someone who has ownership with exclusive rights to something. The owner of a colony has the right to establish a government and distribute land.

Provision – A stock or inventory of goods of needed materials or supplies, as in a food stock.

Publisher – A person or business that publishes (prints and distributes) information, usually in a book or a newspaper.

Quakers – A religious group also known as The Society of Friends. William Penn, a Quaker, established Pennsylvania as a place for Quaker and other settlers to live and freely practice their religious beliefs. He laid out the city of Philadelphia in Pennsylvania. Quakers believe in pacifism.

Quill pen – The hollow, horny shaft of a feather which is used, with ink, to write on paper.

Raft – A group of logs fastened together to transport over water.

Rampart – A protective barrier, a wall-like ridge made of rock, earth, and debris to block passage.

Record – Something that records or writes down in a document evidence of what has happened.

Reservoir – A place where water is collected and stored for use.

Retreat – To move backwards.

Reveille – A signal, like a bugle, calling to make a military (army) formation (grouping and movement).

Revenue – Money that a political group collects (as taxes) into a treasury for public use.

Revolutionary War – The American war that American Colonists fought against Great Britain (England) to become the free, independent country of the United States of America.

Saddler – Someone who makes and repairs or sells saddles and other furnishings to ride animals, usually horses.

Sail – A piece of fabric used with the wind to propel a ship through the water.

Sand-bar – A ridge of sand under water that has been built by currents in a river or other body of water.

Scythe – A tool used for mowing grass made of a long curved blade fastened at an angle to a long handle.

Settlement – The act of settling or giving possession under legal sanction.

Settler – One who colonizes a region.

Shell Corn – To pop kernels of corn off of a corn cob.

Small pox – An acute infectious disease that affects people with skin eruptions and fevers.

Spring Thaw – Elevation of ground water after snow melts in the springtime.

Squatter – One who settles on land without permission, who does not pay rent or purchase for the land.

Stagecoach – A horse drawn passenger and mail coach moving on a regular schedule between established stops.

Steamboat – A boat driven by steam power.

Steer man – Person who controls the course, or direction of a boat or car by using a rudder or wheel to guide or navigate.

Survey – To collect data and mathematically analyze the form, extent and position of a tract of land.

Surveyor – Someone who conducts a survey and makes a map of his findings.

Tanner/Currier – Someone who cleans, tans and treats animal hides to be made into useful leather objects.

Tarred and Feathered – The act of pouring tar onto a person and then dumping feathers to stick onto the tar. This was done in Colonial times to punish people for extreme crimes.

Teamster – One who drives a team of horses, or a truck.

Territory – A geographic area belonging to an authority or government.

Tinner – A tinsmith who makes or repairs things made of sheet metal (thin forms of white metal).

Tomahawk – A light ax thrown as a weapon and also used by hand.

Veteran Soldier – An old soldier who has retired from active duty.

Water Pressure – The force of water moving through a pipe.

Volunteer Fire Company – An organized group of people that volunteers to fight fires in their community without being paid to do this job.

Wheelwright – A maker and repairer of wheels and wheeled vehicles.

Whitesmith – A tinsmith worker in white metal who finishes or polishes the work.

Wooden Type – Type made of wood that is carved into letters. These are then used in a hand printing press to print ink onto paper.

Bibliography

1 Stoll, George. "Map of the 13 Colonies." Hammond Inc. 1967. <http://www.civics-online.org>.

2 Rosenbloom, Joshua. "Indentured Servitude in the Colonial U.S." University of Kansas. March 16, 2008. <http://www.eh.net/encyclopedia/article/Rosenbloom. Indenture>.

3 Tunis, Edward. *Colonial Living.* NY, NY: Thomas Y. Crowell Co., 1957: 78-81.

Also

Barker, Deanna. "Indentured Servitude in Colonial America." Frontier Resources. <http://www.Mert-sahinogly.com/research/indentured-servitude-colonial-america>.

4 Rosenbloom, Joshua. "Indentured Servitude in the Colonial U.S." University of Kansas. March 16, 2008. <http://www.eh.net/encyclopedia/article/Rosenbloom. Indenture>.

5 Jordon, Don and Walsh, Michael. *White Cargo: The Forgotten History of Britain's White Slaves in America.* Washington Square, NY: NY University Press, 2007: 89.

6 Polk, William. *Birth of America from before Columbus to the Revolution.* New York, NY: Harper Perennial, 2007: 234.

7 Jordon, Don and Walsh, Michael. *White Cargo: The Forgotten History of Britain's White Slaves in America.* Washington Square, NY: NY University Press, 2007: 12-13.

8 Polk, William. *Birth of America from before Columbus to the Revolution.* New York, NY: Harper Perennial, 2007: 234.

9 Wright, J.E. and Corbett, Doris S. *Pioneer Life in Western Pennsylvania.* Pittsburgh, PA: University of Pittsburgh Press, 1940: 2-4.

10 Tunis, Edward. *Colonial Living.* NY,NY: Thomas Y. Crowell Co., 1957: 79.

11 Hawke, David Freeman. *Benjamin Franklin.* Koneckly and Koneckly, 1976: 10-11.

12 O'Meara, Walter. *Guns at the Forks.* Pittsburgh, PA: University of Pittsburgh Press, 1979: 46.

13 O'Meara, Walter. *Guns at the Forks.* Pittsburgh, PA: University of Pittsburgh Press, 1979: 46.

14 Morgan, Robert. *Boone: A Biography.* Chapel Hill, NC: Algonquin Books, 2007: 19.

15 "Lacrosse." <http://www.en.wikipedia.org/wiki/La-crosse>.

16 Buck, Solon J. and Buck, Elizabeth Hawthorne. *The Planting of Civilization in Western Pennsylvania.* Pittsburgh, PA: University of Pittsburgh Press, 1939: 43, 54, 55, 60-65, 70-71.

17 Polk, William. *Birth of America from before Columbus to the Revolution.* New York, NY: Harper Perennial, 2007: 220.

18 Polk, William. *Birth of America from before Columbus to the Revolution.* New York, NY: Harper Perennial, 2007: 221.

19 O'Meara, Walter. *Guns at the Forks.* Pittsburgh, PA: University of Pittsburgh Press, 1979: 26.

20 Gaff, Alan D. *Bayonets in the Wilderness, Anthony Wayne's Legion in the Old Northwest.* University of Oklahoma Press, 2004: 70.

21 Buck, Solon J. and Buck, Elizabeth Hawthorne. *The Planting of Civilization in Western Pennsylvania.* Pittsburgh, PA: University of Pittsburgh Press, 1939: 29, 72.

22 Alberts, Robert C. *Hardships and Heroics: Southwestern Pennsylvania, 1749-1799.* Pittsburgh National Bank Bicentennnial Celebration Commission, 1975: 4.

23 "ExplorePAhistory.com Historical Markers: Queen Aliquippa." <http://www.ExplorePAhistory.com/hmarker.php?markerID=746>.

24 Frey, Laura C. *The Land in the Fork, Pittsburgh 1753-1914.,* Philadelphia, PA: Dorrance and Company, 1955: 11.

25 Wright, J.E. and Corbett, Doris S. *Pioneer Life in Western Pennsylvania.* Pittsburgh, PA: University of Pittsburgh Press, 1940: 30.

Also

Lorant, Stefan. *Pittsburgh, the Story of an American City.* NY,NY: Doubleday and Company, 1964: 17-19

Also

Kinnaird, Clark. George Washington, The Pictorial Biography. New York: Hastings House Publishers, Inc., 1967: 24-27.

26   Hawke, David Freeman. *Benjamin Franklin*. Koneckly and Koneckly, 1976: 139.

27   Buck, Solon J. and Buck, Elizabeth Hawthorne. *The Planting of Civilization in Western Pennsylvania. Pittsburgh, PA:*University of Pittsburgh Press, 1939: 165-174.

28   Lorant, Stefan. *Pittsburgh, the Story of an American City.* Garden City, NY: Doubleday and Company, 1964: 46.

29   Kinnaird, Clark. George Washington, The Pictorial Biography. New York: Hastings House Publishers, Inc., 1967: 28-29.

Also

    Buck, Solon J. and Buck, Elizabeth Hawthorne. *The Planting of Civilization in Western Pennsylvania. Pittsburgh, PA:* University of Pittsburgh Press, 1939: 74-86.

Also

    Baldwin, Leland D. *Pittsburgh, the Story of a City.* Pittsburgh, PA: University of Pittsburgh Press: 1937: 27-37.

30   Hawke, David Freeman. *Benjamin Franklin*. Koneckly and Koneckly, 1976: 99, 113, 153-154, 207-208.

31   Kummerow, O'Toole and Stephenson. *Pennsylvania's Forbes Trail. NY,NY:* Taylor Trade Publishing, 2008: 122.

32   Wright, J.E. and Corbett, Doris S. *Pioneer Life in Western Pennsylvania*. Pittsburgh, PA: University of Pittsburgh Press, 1940: 33.

33   Galley, Henrietta and Arnold, J.O. *History of the Galley Family with Local and Old Time Sketches in the Yough Region.* Greensburg, PA: P.C. Henry Print Company, 1968: 300.

34   Wallace, Paul A.W. *Indian Paths of Pennsylvania.* Harrisburg, PA:The Pennsylvania Historical and Museum Commission, 1965.

35   Wright, J.E. and Corbett, Doris S. *Pioneer Life in Western Pennsylvania*. Pittsburgh, PA: University of Pittsburgh Press, 1940: 175-182.

36   Morgan, Robert. *Boone: A Biography.* Chapel Hill, NC: Algonquin Books, 2007: 134.

37   Baldwin, Leland D. *Pittsburgh, the Story of a City.* Pittsburgh, PA: University of Pittsburgh Press: 1937: 137.

38   Boucher, John Newton. "Traveling Eastward: Quick Transportation. A Century and a half of Pittsburgh and Her People." The Lewis Publishing Co., 1908. <http://www.clpgh.org/research/pittsburgh/history/pgh1816.html>.

39   McElhaney, Marie. "The Swearingen Conestoga Wagon." Milestones Vol. 22, No. 4, Winter 1997 <http://www.bchistory.org/beavercounty/beavercountytopical/transportation/ConewtogaMW97.html>.

40   McElhaney, Marie. "The Swearingen Conestoga Wagon." Milestones Vol. 22, No. 4, Winter 1997 <http://www.bchistory.org/beavercounty/beavercountytopical/transportation/ConewtogaMW97.html>.

41   "The Conestoga Wagon." Conestoga Area Historical Society, P 3. <http://www.rootsweb.ancestry.com/~pacahs/wagon.html>.

42   Boucher, John Newton. "Traveling Eastward: Quick Transportation. A Century and a half of Pittsburgh and Her People." The Lewis Publishing Co., 1908. <http://www.clpgh.org/research/pittsburgh/history/pgh1816.html>.

Also

    Frey, Laura C. *The Land in the Fork, Pittsburgh 1753-1914.,* Philadelphia, PA: Dorrance and Company, 1955: 30-31.

43   Lorant, Stefan. *Pittsburgh, the Story of an American City.* Garden City, NY: Doubleday and Company, 1964: 32.

44   Lorant, Stefan. *Pittsburgh, the Story of an American City.* Garden City, NY: Doubleday and Company, 1964: 38.

45   O'Meara, Walter. *Guns at the Forks.* Pittsburgh, PA: University of Pittsburgh Press, 1979: 219-223.

46   Stotz, Charles M. *Drums in the Forest, Defense in the Wilderness.* The Historical Society of Western Pennsylvania. Pittsburgh, PA: University of Pittsburgh Press, 1958: 161-162.

47   Morgan, Robert. *Boone: A Biography.* Chapel Hill, NC: Algonquin Books, 2007: 23.

48   Dixon, David. *Fort Pitt Museum, Pennsylvania Trail of History Guide.* Mechanicsburg, PA: Stackpole Books, 2004: 32.

Also

    "Guyasuta." <http://www.en.wikipedia.org/wiki/Guyasuta>.

49   Dixon, David. *Fort Pitt Museum, Pennsylvania Trail of History Guide.* Mechanicsburg, PA: Stackpole Books, 2004: 30.

Also

    Bouquet, Henry. "The papers of Henry Bouquet," Ed. S.K. Stevens, Donald H. Kent, Autumn Leonard. The Pennsylvania Historical and Museum Commission. Harrisburg, PA, 1951, Vol. 6, Letter of Ecuyer dated 2 June 1763: 202.

50   Slick, Sewell Elias. *William Trent and the West.* Lewisburg, PA: Wennawoods Publishing, 2001: 111-112.

51   Stotz, Charles M. *Drums in the Forest, Defense in the Wilderness.* The Historical Society of Western Pennsylvania. Pittsburgh, PA: University of Pittsburgh Press, 1958: 176.

52   Bouquet, Henry. "The papers of Henry Bouquet," Ed. S.K. Stevens, Donald H. Kent, Autumn Leonard. The Pennsylvania Historical and Museum Commission. Harrisburg, PA, 1951, Vol. 6, Letter of Bouquet to Amherst dated 11 August 1763: 361.

53   Edkert, Allan W. *The Conquerors, Narratives of America, Book II.* New York, NY: Bantam Books, 1970: 478-481.

54   Dixon, David. *Fort Pitt Museum, Pennsylvania Trail of History Guide.* Mechanicsburg, PA: Stackpole Books, 2004: 32.

55   Edkert, Allan W. *The Conquerors, Narratives of America, Book II.* New York, NY: Bantam Books, 1970: 599-609.

56 "Mary Schenley." <http://www.en.wkikpedia.org/wiki/ Mary_Schenley>.

57 Dahlinger, Charles W. *Pittsburgh, a Sketch of Its Early Social Life.* New York: Knickerbocker Press, 1916: 33.

58 Lorant, Stefan. *Pittsburgh, the Story of an American City.* Garden City, NY: Doubleday and Company, 1964: 44.

59 Wilson, Erasmus. *History of Pittsburg.* Chicago, IL: H.R. Cornell and Co., 1898: 63.

60 Dahlinger, Charles W. *Pittsburgh, a Sketch of Its Early Social Life.* New York: Knickerbocker Press, 1916: 33-35.

61 Baldwin, Leland D. *Pittsburgh, the Story of a City.* Pittsburgh, PA: University of Pittsburgh Press, 1937: 134.

62 Dahlinger, Charles W. *Pittsburgh, a Sketch of Its Early Social Life.* New York: Knickerbocker Press, 1916: 161-183.

63 Henry, Charles. *A History of Transportation in the Ohio Valley.* Glendale, CA: The Arthur H. Clark Company, 1932: 41-42.

64 Baldwin, Leland D. *Pittsburgh, the Story of a City.* Pittsburgh, PA: University of Pittsburgh Press, 1937: 132.

65 Henry, Charles. *A History of Transportation in the Ohio Valley.* Glendale, CA: The Arthur H. Clark Company, 1932: 74.

66 Lorant, Stefan. *Pittsburgh, the Story of an American City.* Garden City, NY: Doubleday and Company, 1964: 49.

67 Lorant, Stefan. *Pittsburgh, the Story of an American City.* Garden City, NY: Doubleday and Company, 1964: 52.

68 Dahlinger, Charles W. *Pittsburgh, a Sketch of Its Early Social Life.* New York: Knickerbocker Press, 1916: 29-30.

69 Wright, J.E. and Corbett, Doris S. *Pioneer Life in Western Pennsylvania.* Pittsburgh, PA: University of Pittsburgh Press, 1940: 220.

70 Buck, Solon J. and Buck, Elizabeth Hawthorne. *The Planting of Civilization in Western Pennsylvania.* Pittsburgh, PA: University of Pittsburgh Press, 1939: 308.

71 Dahlinger, Charles W. *Pittsburgh, a Sketch of Its Early Social Life.* New York: Knickerbocker Press, 1916: 29-17.

Also

Lorant, Stefan. *Pittsburgh, the Story of an American City.* Garden City, NY: Doubleday and Company, 1964: 63.

72 Lorant, Stefan. *Pittsburgh, the Story of an American City.* Garden City, NY: Doubleday and Company, 1964: 460.

73 Wright, J.E. and Corbett, Doris S. *Pioneer Life in Western Pennsylvania.* Pittsburgh, PA: University of Pittsburgh Press, 1940: 64-69.

Also

Lorant, Stefan. *Pittsburgh, the Story of an American City.* Garden City, NY: Doubleday and Company, 1964: 50.

74 Wright, J.E. and Corbett, Doris S. *Pioneer Life in Western Pennsylvania.* Pittsburgh, PA: University of Pittsburgh Press, 1940: 94-95.

Also

Lorant, Stefan. *Pittsburgh, the Story of an American City.* Garden City, NY: Doubleday and Company, 1964: 50.

75 Morgan, Robert. *Boone: A Biography.* Chapel Hill, NC: Algonquin Books, 2007: 62.

76 Buck, Solon J. and Buck, Elizabeth Hawthorne. *The Planting of Civilization in Western Pennsylvania.* Pittsburgh, PA: University of Pittsburgh Press, 1939: 392.

77 Sloane, Eric. *Diary of an Early American Boy: Noah Blake 1805.* New York: Ballantine Books, 1965: 6.

78 Frey, Laura C. *The Land in the Fork, Pittsburgh 1753-1914.,* Philadelphia, PA: Dorrance and Company, 1955: 56-59.

79 Galley, Henrietta and Arnold, J.O. *History of the Galley Family with Local and Old Time Sketches in the Yough Region.* Greensburg, PA: P.C. Henry Print Company, 1968: 333-336.

80 Norcross, Eric. "Cordless Toasters. An Over-view of Non-Electric Toasters." <http://www.toaster.org/museum.html>.

81 Burnston, Sharon Ann. *Fitting & Proper, 18th Century Clothing from the Collection of the Chester County Historical Society.* Texarkana, Texas: Southwest Printers & Publishers, March 2000: 115.

82 Baldwin, Leland D. *Pittsburgh, the Story of a City.* Pittsburgh, PA: University of Pittsburgh Press, 1937: 135.

83 Henry, Charles. *A History of Transportation in the Ohio Valley.* Glendale, CA: The Arthur H. Clark Company, 1932: 42-43.

84 Baldwin, Leland D. *Pittsburgh, the Story of a City.* Pittsburgh, PA: University of Pittsburgh Press, 1937: 139.

85 Baldwin, Leland D. *Pittsburgh, the Story of a City.* Pittsburgh, PA: University of Pittsburgh Press, 1937: 130-140.

86 Perrin, William H. "The Pioneer Days of Old-Time Keelboats– 1890." <http://www.kentuckyexployer.com/ nonmembers/01-04035.html>.

87 Sutcliffe, Andrea. *Steam, The Untold Story of America's First Great Invention.* Ny, NY: Palgrave Macmillan, 2004: 1-180.

88 Demorest, Rose. *Pittsburgh, A Bicentennial Tribute 1758-1958. Carnegie Library of Pittsburgh 1958.* Pennsylvania Department. <http://www.clpgh.org/ research/pittsburgh/history/demorest.html>.

Also

Buck, Solon J. and Buck, Elizabeth Hawthorne. *The Planting of Civilization in Western Pennsylva* Pittsburgh, PA: University of Pittsburgh Press, 19 250.

89 Baldwin, Leland D. *Pittsburgh, the Story of a C* Pittsburgh, PA: University of Pittsburgh Press 189-191.

90   Baldwin, Leland D. *Pittsburgh, the Story of a City*. Pittsburgh, PA: University of Pittsburgh Press, 1937: 136.

91   Lorant, Stefan. *Pittsburgh, the Story of an American City*. Garden City, NY: Doubleday and Company, 1964: 69.

Also

"Mike Fink, Historical figure." <http://en.wikipedia.org/wiki/Mike_Fink>.

92   Field, Timothy. "Mike Fink: The Last of the Boatmen." <http://xroads.virginia.edu/~HYPER/DETOC/sw/fink6.html>.

93   Gaff, Alan D. *Bayonets in the Wilderness, Anthony Wayne's Legion in the Old Northwest*. Oklahoma: University of Oklahoma Press, 2004: 70.

Also

Hogeland, William. *The Whiskey Rebellion*. A Lisa Drew Book. NY, NY:Scribner, 2006: 140.

94   "Northwest Territory from Conservapedia." < http://www.conservapedia.com/Northwest_Territory>.

Also

Buck, Solon J. and Buck, Elizabeth Hawthorne. *The Planting of Civilization in Western Pennsylvania*. Pittsburgh, PA: University of Pittsburgh Press, 1939: 202-203.

Gaff, Alan D. *Bayonets in the Wilderness, Anthony Wayne's Legion in the Old Northwest*. Oklahoma: University of Oklahoma Press, 2004: 365.

n, Leland D. *Pittsburgh, the Story of a City*. , PA: University of Pittsburgh Press, 1937:

and Museum. reciationLandsMuseum.org>.

Land Speculation, History n.wikipedia.org/wiki/

deral Writers' Project, William Penn As-

99   Swell, Barbara. *Log Cabin Cooking*. Asheville, NC: Native Ground Music, Inc., 1996: 16.

100 Swell, Barbara. *Log Cabin Cooking*. Asheville, NC: Native Ground Music, Inc., 1996: 15.

101 Wright, J.E. and Corbett, Doris S. *Pioneer Life in Western Pennsylvania*. Pittsburgh, PA: University of Pittsburgh Press, 1940: 39-40.

102 Lorant, Stefan. *Pittsburgh, the Story of an American City*. Garden City, NY: Doubleday and Company, 1964: 56-57.

103 Lorant, Stefan. *Pittsburgh, the Story of an American City*. Garden City, NY: Doubleday and Company, 1964: 56.

104 Ambrose, Stephen E. *Undaunted Courage*. Touchstone Book. NY, NY: Simon & Schuster, 1996: 38-41.

Also

Lorant, Stefan. *Pittsburgh, the Story of an American City*. Garden City, NY: Doubleday and Company, 1964: 71.

105 Hogeland, William. *The Whiskey Rebellion*. A Lisa Drew Book. NY, NY: Scribner, 2006: 99-100.

106 Hogeland, William. *The Whiskey Rebellion*. A Lisa Drew Book. NY, NY: Scribner, 2006: 152-154.

107 Knight, David C. *The Whiskey Rebellion, 1794*. New York, NY: Franklin Watts, Inc., 1968: 45.

108 Dahlinger, Charles W. *Pittsburgh, a Sketch of Its Early Social Life*. New York: Knickerbocker Press, 1916: 81.

109 Ambrose, Stephen E. *Undaunted Courage*. Touchstone Book. NY, NY: Simon & Schuster, 1996: 41.

110 Davis, Kenneth C. *Don't know much about History*. NY, NY: HarperCollins Publishers, 2003: 148.

111 Ambrose, Stephen E. *Undaunted Courage*. Touchstone Book. NY, NY: Simon & Schuster, 1996: 39.

112 Gragg, Rod. *Lewis and Clark on the Trail of Discovery, the Journey that Shaped America*. Nashville, Tennessee: Rutledge Hill Press, 2003: 8-44.

113 "Main Line of Public Works." <http://wapedia.mobi/en/Pennsylvania_Main_Line_of_Public_Works>.

Also

Bourne, Russell. *Floating West, The Erie and Other American Canals*. NY, NY: W.W. Norton & Co., 1992: 183, 199-206.

114 Lewie, Chris J. "The Allegheny Portage Railroad (Pennsylvania, USA)." *Funimag, the first web magazine about funiculars*. Ed. Michel Azema. <http://www.funimag.com/funimag28/Allegheny01.htm>.

115 McCullough, David. *The Great Bridge. NY, NY:* Simon & Schuster, 1982: 48-49.

116 "American Canal Society." <http://www.americancanals.org/Pennsylvania/Western%20Div%20PA3.pdf>.

117 Boucher, John Newton. *A Century and a half of Pittsburg and her people, Chapter XXX*. New York: The Lewis Publishing Company, 1908.

118 Lorant, Stefan. *Pittsburgh, the Story of an American City*. Garden City, NY: Doubleday and Company, 1964: 121.

119 McCullough, David. *The Great Bridge. NY, NY:* Simon & Schuster, 1982: 64-65.

120 "Pennsylvania Canal." *Absolute Astronomy.com@2009.* <http://www.absoluteastronomy.com/topcis/Pennsylvania_Canal>.

Also

"Stories from PA History, Crossing the Alleghenies, Chapter Three: Pennsylvania Canal and Railroad." <http://explorepahistory.com/story.php?storyId=10&chapter=4>.

121 Thurston, George H. *Pittsburgh It's History and Resources*. Pittsburgh, PA: AA Anderson & Son, 1886: 57.

122 Bining, Arthur Cecil. *Pennsylvania Iron Manufacture in the Eighteenth Century*. Pennsylvania Historical and Museum Commission, Harrisburg, PA, 1973: 57-58.

123 Lorant, Stefan. *Pittsburgh, the Story of an American City*. Garden City, NY: Doubleday and Company, 1964: 70.

124 Bining, Arthur Cecil. *Pennsylvania Iron Manufacture in the Eighteenth Century*. Pennsylvania Historical and Museum Commission, Harrisburg, PA, 1973: 63.

125 Bining, Arthur Cecil. *Pennsylvania Iron Manufacture in the Eighteenth Century.* Pennsylvania Historical and Museum Commission, Harrisburg, PA, 1973: 62.

126 Bining, Arthur Cecil. *Pennsylvania Iron Manufacture in the Eighteenth Century.* Pennsylvania Historical and Museum Commission, Harrisburg, PA, 1973: 59.

127 Bining, Arthur Cecil. *Pennsylvania Iron Manufacture in the Eighteenth Century.* Pennsylvania Historical and Museum Commission, Harrisburg, PA, 1973: 68.

128 Glasco, Laurence A., et al. *Free at Last? Slavery in Pittsburgh in the 18th and 19th Centuries. Pittsburgh, PA:* University of Pittsburgh Publication for an exhibition at the Senator John Heinz History Center, 2008-2009: 3-4.

129 *WPA History of the Negro in Pittsburgh.* Ed. Lawrence Glasco. Pittsburgh, PA: University of Pittsburgh Press, 2004: 54, 56-57.

130 *WPA History of the Negro in Pittsburgh.* Ed. Lawrence Glasco. Pittsburgh, PA: University of Pittsburgh Press, 2004: 54, 56-89.

131 *Forging Ahead, Pittsburgh at 250.* Ed. Richard A. Monti and Sandra Skowron. *Pittsburgh, PA:* Tribune Review Publishing Co, 2008: 38.

132 *WPA History of the Negro in Pittsburgh.* Ed. Lawrence Glasco. Pittsburgh, PA: University of Pittsburgh Press, 2004: 44.

133 *WPA History of the Negro in Pittsburgh.* Ed. Lawrence Glasco. Pittsburgh, PA: University of Pittsburgh Press, 2004: 46.

134 Dahlinger, Charles W. *Pittsburgh, a Sketch of Its Early Social Life.* New York: Knickerbocker Press, 1916:39.

135 "The Pittsburgh Great Fire of April 10, 1845." *Allegheny Cemetery Heritage, Pittsburgh, PA, Fall, 2009:* 4-6, 12.

136 "The Great Fire." *The Pittsburgh Automobilist Automobile Club of Pittsburgh.* Ed. Paul C. Wolff. Albany, NY: JB Lyon Company, May, 1937.

Also

Link, Gary. *The Burnt District.* Baltimore, MD: PublishAmerica Book Publishers, 2003: 1-17.

137 "The Great Fire." *The Pittsburgh Automobilist Automobile Club of Pittsburgh.* Ed. Paul C. Wolff. Albany, NY: JB Lyon Company, May, 1937.

Also

Lorant, Stefan. *Pittsburgh, the Story of an American City.* Garden City, NY: Doubleday and Company, 1964: 110-111.

138 Starrett, Agnes Lynch. *Through One Hundred Fifty Years: The University of Pittsburgh.* Pittsburgh, PA: University of Pittsburgh Press, 1937: 109-111.

139 Hoffert, Sylvia D. *Jane Grey Swisshelm, An Unconventional Life 1815-1884.* Chapel Hill, NC: University of North Carolina Press, 2004: 67.

140 Dahlinger, Charles W. *Pittsburgh, a Sketch of Its Early Social Life.* New York: Knickerbocker Press, 1916: 142-149.

141 Dahlinger, Charles W. *Pittsburgh, a Sketch of Its Early Social Life.* New York: Knickerbocker Press, 1916: 15-16.

142 Dahlinger, Charles W. *Pittsburgh, a Sketch of Its Early Social Life.* New York: Knickerbocker Press, 1916: 55-63.

Also

Baldwin, Leland D. *Pittsburgh, the Story of a City.* Pittsburgh, PA: University of Pittsburgh Press, 1937: 111-114.

143 Dahlinger, Charles W. *Pittsburgh, a Sketch of Its Early Social Life.* New York: Knickerbocker Press, 1916: 48.

144 Dahlinger, Charles W. *Pittsburgh, a Sketch of Its Early Social Life.* New York: Knickerbocker Press, 1916:32.

145 Baldwin, Leland D. *Pittsburgh, the Story of a City.* Pittsburgh, PA: University of Pittsburgh Press, 1937: 148-149.

Also

Dahlinger, Charles W. *Pittsburgh, a Sketch of Its Early Social Life.* New York: Knickerbocker Press, 1916: 78.

Also

Frey, Laura C. *The Land in the Fork, Pittsburgh 1753-1914,* Philadelphia, PA: Dorrance and Company, 1955: 65-75.

146 Dahlinger, Charles W. *Pittsburgh, a Sketch of Its Early Social Life.* New York: Knickerbocker Press, 1916:40-41.

147 Dahlinger, Charles W. *Pittsburgh, a Sketch of Its Early Social Life.* New York: Knickerbocker Press, 1916: 56, 75.

Also

Buck, Solon J. and Buck, Elizabeth Hawthorne. *The Planting of Civilization in Western Pennsylvania. Pittsburgh, PA:* University of Pittsburgh Press, 1939: 255.

148 Buck, Solon J. and Buck, Elizabeth Hawthorne. *The Planting of Civilization in Western Pennsylvania. Pittsburgh, PA:* University of Pittsburgh Press, 1939: 189-190.

Also

Baldwin, Leland D. *Pittsburgh, the Story of a City.* Pittsburgh, PA: University of Pittsburgh Press: 1937: 93.

149 Dahlinger, Charles W. *Pittsburgh, a Sketch of Its Early Social Life.* New York: Knickerbocker Press, 1916: 41.

150 Dahlinger, Charles W. *Pittsburgh, a Sketch of Its Early Social Life.* New York: Knickerbocker Press, 1916: 50-57, 131-132.

151 Dahlinger, Charles W. *Pittsburgh, a Sketch of Its Early Social Life.* New York: Knickerbocker Press, 1916: 41.

Also

Baldwin, Leland D. *Pittsburgh, the Story of a City.* Pittsburgh, PA: University of Pittsburgh Press: 1937: 162.

Time Line

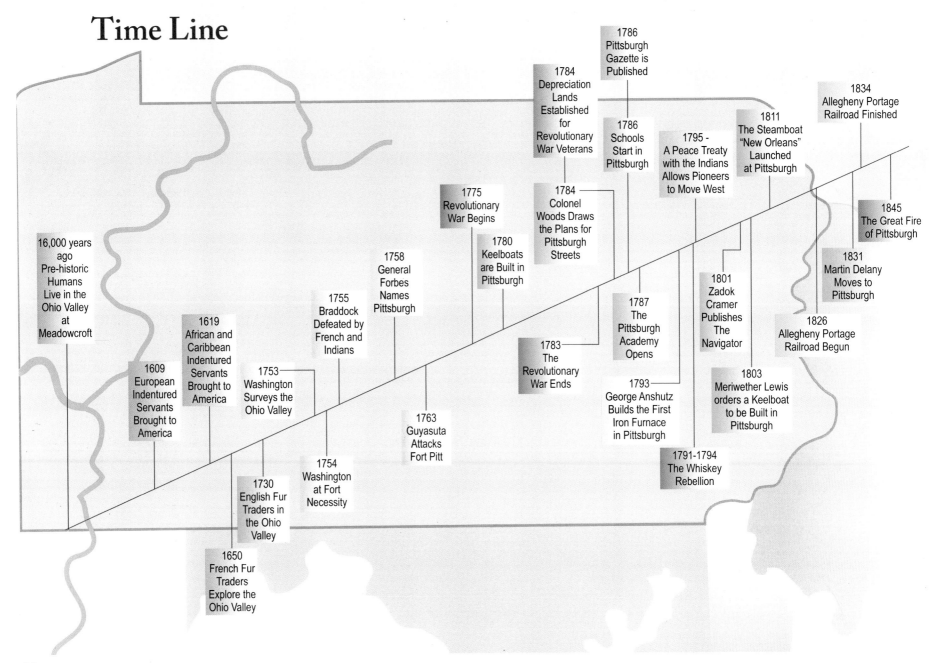

16,000 years ago
Pre-historic Humans Live in the Ohio Valley at Meadowcroft

1609
European Indentured Servants Brought to America

1619
African and Caribbean Indentured Servants Brought to America

1650
French Fur Traders Explore the Ohio Valley

1730
English Fur Traders in the Ohio Valley

1753
Washington Surveys the Ohio Valley

1754
Washington at Fort Necessity

1755
Braddock Defeated by French and Indians

1758
General Forbes Names Pittsburgh

1763
Guyasuta Attacks Fort Pitt

1775
Revolutionary War Begins

1780
Keelboats are Built in Pittsburgh

1783
The Revolutionary War Ends

1784
Depreciation Lands Established for Revolutionary War Veterans

1784
Colonel Woods Draws the Plans for Pittsburgh Streets

1786
Pittsburgh Gazette is Published

1786
Schools Start in Pittsburgh

1787
The Pittsburgh Academy Opens

1793
George Anshutz Builds the First Iron Furnace in Pittsburgh

1795 -
A Peace Treaty with the Indians Allows Pioneers to Move West

1791-1794
The Whiskey Rebellion

1801
Zadok Cramer Publishes The Navigator

1803
Meriwether Lewis orders a Keelboat to be Built in Pittsburgh

1811
The Steamboat "New Orleans" Launched at Pittsburgh

1826
Allegheny Portage Railroad Begun

1831
Martin Delany Moves to Pittsburgh

1834
Allegheny Portage Railroad Finished

1845
The Great Fire of Pittsburgh